THE FLEET AIR ARM SONG BOOK

THE FLEET AIR ARM
SONG BOOK

For Private Circulation only

PREFACE TO THE MARK II EDITION

The opportunity to make a chronological arrangement has been taken with this second edition of the Songbook. An alphabetical order had some advantages, but it was felt that the songs, more specifically, the flying songs, represent a quite unique record of nearly seventy years of all the varying forms of naval aviation, particularly the temporary problems and preoccupations of those at the sharp end, and in a way that no official volume could quite achieve. Even more, they provide an insight into the character and some of the unchanging aspects of the outlook of naval aviators brought together by the Association, whether split-arse over Cambrai in 1914—18, exercising in the Med. between the wars, striking Taranto or pranging Barracudas in 1939—45, dodging the Korean flak in the 1950's, fighting from choppers over the Malayan jungle in the 1960's, or, more than a decade later, hovering in a Force Eight over stricken oil rigs, or landing several tons of high-speed Phantom on board **Ark Royal.**

Therefore, the book has been split into sections corresponding to the flying songs of the R.N.A.S. and Fleet Air Arm over the years. The other songs and occasional recitations and set-pieces that have proved popular round the Wardroom piano have been separately grouped at the back of the book, and alphabetically arranged under the main headings of General Odes and Ditties, and their Naval and Military equivalents. In response to appeals many FAAOA members sent songs not included in the Songbook Mk. 1 Particularly, there was a gratifying and large contribution of modern songs, and, surprisingly, no fewer than thirty-odd 'new' wartime numbers not only of 1939—45, but also of 1914—18 vintage. As a result, something had to give. A number of songs that appeared in the original Songbook have therefore had to be scrapped. These, mainly, were songs that can easily be found in the Youth Hostels Songbook (e.g. *Widecombe Fair, Ilkley Moor* etc.) and some of the more esoteric and obscure ditties belonging, perhaps, more to Saturday night at the Rugger Club than Dining-in Night on board. Obviously, a few members will find that their particular favourite from Songbook Mk.I has vanished. In such cases, sufficient pressure in the right quarters might ensure re-instatement in the event of a Songbook Mk.III. Otherwise, it is, to quote a popular F.A.A. mode of address: 'Ard Luck. Equally, amendments have been made to various lines and, in some cases, entire songs, and it is recognised that not everyone is guaranteed to be pleased by the result; nevertheless, the aim has been to try and secure a version in each instance that is acceptable to a majority. At the same time, it is regretted that it has still proved impossible to identify by name several of the traditional tunes to which some songs are sung.

Thanks are finally due to the well-known but anonymous editor of the Songbook Mk.I on whose splendid hard work this edition is very broadly based, and, once again, to Tugg for the superb cartoons; also to all the FAAOA members who kindly sent their songs, songbooks, suggestions and amendments, and, as a whole, gave tremendous support to what is hoped will be seen as a bumper new book. 2

THE A25 SONG

(TUNE: Villikins and his Dinah)

If the Fleet Air Arm has a hymn, although that is not quite the
correct term, this is it: sung in the Ward rooms of every carrier
and naval air station all over the world over the years in many
varying forms; but always with the chorus paying tribute to the
ability to sign the Accident Form A25. The original Song Book
had 13 verses; now, very appropriately, 25 have been found,
including the original version written in Cabin 75, in the Arab
Quarter of HMS Formidable 1942/43 by David A. Wright of 893
Squadron and Derek Stevenson. Since then, deserved popularity
and constant repetitions have resulted in scores of small
variations in the lines, some changing of the original (particularly
verse 3, first line), as well as many additions, right up to the 1970's
with Phantoms and Buccaneers. A separate Rotary Wing version
exists, to be found later in the book. It proved impossible in
editing to provide every textual variation. The version printed
below includes much of the original (some verses of which did
not become as popular as others) and the best that could be done
to arrive at a full, acceptable, and reasonably well-known form of
words. Anyone whose own particular favourite version does not
quite coincide will have to amend accordingly.

1   I'll sing you a song about sailors who fly,
       A *Formidable* Fleet Air Arm pilot am I
       I've seized up 'em all — Merlins, Cyclones and Taurus
       And many's the time that I've chanted this chorus.....

CHORUS (between each verse)
    Cracking show, I'm alive,
    But I've still got to render my A25.

2.   They say in the Air Force a landing's okay,
      If the pilot gets out and can still walk away,
      But in the Fleet Air Arm the prospects are dim
      If the landing's piss poor and the pilot can't swim.

3.   I fly for a living, and not just for fun,
      I'm not awfully anxious to hack down the Hun,
      And as for deck-landings at night in the dark,
      As I told Wings this morning, 'Fuck that for a lark.'

4.   Tail up down the flight deck to do an umbrella
      I remember too late to fine pitch the propellor,
      So I stamp on the wheel brakes and then get the shits,
      As the whole bloody issue goes arse over tits.

5.   When the batsman gives 'Lower' I always go higher,
      I drift off to starboard and prang my Seafire,
      The boys in the Goofers all think that I'm green,
      But I get my commission from Supermarine.

6.   I sat on the booster, awaiting the kick,
Amusing myself by rotating the stick,
Down went the green flag, the engine went 'Cough',
'Cor blimey' said Wings, 'He has tossed himself off.'

7.   As I roar down the flight-deck in my Martlet Mark IV,
Loud in my ears is the Cyclone's sweet roar,
Chuff clank clink, chuff clank clink, chuff clink clink clink,
Away wing on pom pom, away life in drink.

8.   I thought I was coming in low enough but,
I was fifty feet up when the batsman gave 'Cut',
And loud in my earoles the sweet angels sang,
Float, float, float, float, float, float... Barrier... PRANG!

9.   If you come o'er the round-down and see Wings's frown,
You can safely assume that your hook isn't down,
A bloody great barrier looms up in front,
And you hear Wings's shout 'Cut your engine – you cunt.'

10.   They gave me a Seafire to beat up the Fleet,
I polished off the Nelson and Rodney a treat,
But then I forgot the high mast on Formid,
And a seat in the Goofers was worth fifty quid.

11.   When ever I land on I haven't a care,
I float over wires with my head bowed in prayer,
And whilst evil Goofers chant 'High Tiddly Highty'
I know my redeemer is Christ the Almighty.

12.   No one in their right mind stream lands after me,
They'll have to go round again sure as can be,
'Cos I've found a way to get on to a carrier,
Bugger the batsman, aim straight for the barrier.

13.   Red Leader shouts 'Bandits, in line astern, dive,'
And I flick back the tit guard to make the guns live.
But out of my wings there's a Rat-a-tat-tat',
And Red Leader's last words are 'You stupid great twat.'

14.   When the batsman said take-off I thought I knew how,
I opened the throttle and pissed o'er the bow,
But I wasn't airborne, so pity poor me,
With a fucking great splash I came down in the sea.

15.   My C.O. has promised to lend me a Moth,
A dreadful contraption made of wood, string and cloth,
He says its performance, like mine, is fantastic,
We both go like crazy on knicker elastic.

16.   I flew a Mosquito and got myself lost,
So I had to force-land to find out where I wast,
But small field procedure is not very gut,
With a wing loading 47 pounds per square foot.

17. Forming up on a popsie at Mers el Kebir,
    She veered off to port when I moved in too near,
    When I lined up behind her, she started to spin,
    But with opposite rudder I spun myself in.

18. They sent me to Anthorn with two-and-a-half,
    With nothing to do but sit on my arse,
    For all that I do here I might as well be,
    Back flying Proctors from Worthy to Lee.

19. There's a bloke on our ship now that everyone knows,
    Where he gets his rings from Christ only knows,
    He stands on the bridge and he rants and he shouts,
    And he shouts about things he knows fuckall about.

20. Now that I'm older I cannot complain,
    Because Goering's invented the pilotless plane,
    I sit in the crew room and zizz all the day,
    And this is the song that you'll not hear me say.

21. The latest edition's the bold Buccaneer,
    Filled up with black boxes and Scimitar gear,
    But "never mind Kruschev, you're safe till the days,
    When the fucking great bastard is fitted with Speys".

22. At A/S the Wessex is remarkably sound,
    It's wings don't go out — they go round and around,
    Forwards and backwards and sideways they go,
    And they don't give a fuck if their balls' hanging low.

23. Now if you fly Vixens you've got to be quick,
    'Cos it climbs very fast when you pull back the stick.
    "Oh Christ" said a Pilot as heaven drew near,
    "Pray what do you want? said a voice in his ear,

24. The Phantom is highest and fastest and last,
    For the time is now come when we sing of things past,
    For Wilson and Healey have won in the end.
    And there'll soon be no flat tops for us to defend.

25. The moral of this story is quite plain to see,
    A Fleet Air Arm pilot you never should be,
    But stay on the shore and get two rings or more,
    And go out every night on the piss with a whore.

5

THE BOLD AVIATOR
(TUNE: The Tarpaulin Jacket)

This has the strongest claim to be the oldest flying song of all, irrespective of service. There were many versions and variants throughout the 1914–18 war, and even in the 1939–45 period there was an up-dated form with mention of 20 mm cannon shell and radial engine. But the song was apparently extant as long ago as 1912 when the legendary Commander Samson became the first R.N. aviator to fly off a ship, and this is but one version of it.

Oh the bold aviator was dying,
And as 'neath the wreck-age he lay, he lay,
To the sobbing me-chanics about him
These last parting words he did say:

> *CHORUS*
> *Two valve springs you'll find in my stomach,*
> *Three spark plugs are safe in my lung (my lung),*
> *The prop is in splinters inside me,*
> *To my fingers the joy-stick has clung.*

Oh had I the wings of a little dove,
Far a-way, far a-way would I fly, I fly,
Straight to the arms of my true love,
And there would I lay me and die.

> Take the propellor boss out of my liver,
> Take the aileron out of my thigh (my thigh)
> From the seat of my pants take the piston,
> Then see if the old crate will fly.

Then get you two little white tombstones,
Put them one at my head and my toe , my toe,
And get you a pen-knife and scratch there,
"Here lies a poor pilot below",

> Take the cylinders out of my kidneys,
> The connecting-rod out of my brain (my brain),
> From the small of my back get the crankshaft,
> And assemble the en-gyne again.

And when at the Court of Enquiry
They ask for the reason I died, I died,
Please say I forgot twice iota
Was the minimum angle of glide. Oh –

> Take the cylinders out of my kidneys
> The connecting rod out of my brain (my brain),
> From the small of my back get the crank shaft,
> And assemble the en-gyne again.

THE BIRTH OF THE BLUES

Songs of the R.N.A.S.

Shared with the R.F.C.
1914 - 18

I LEFT THE MESS-ROOM EARLY
(TUNE: Keyhole in the Door)

This very popular song originated with the RNAS squadrons on the Western Front, although eventually there were RFC versions of it which were widely sung.

I left the Mess room early just on the stroke of nine
And greatly to my horror the weather promised fine.
I strolled up to the hangars, those regions to explore.
And found my 'bus all ready, outside the hangar door.

I thought I'd try my engine to see what she would do,
The counter showed eight fifty revs, the cylinders were blue.
The damn thing missed eight fifty times, which made me hold my breath,
As I climbed into the atmosphere to juggle there with death.

At last we reached four thousand feet and met the old F.E.'s,
The morning air was very cold which made my pecker freeze.
And soon we crossed the German lines quite close to old Bapaume,
And as I saw the Archie burst, I thought of Home Sweet Home.

The F.E.s they went Eastward, followed by the Pups,
And by the time we reached Cambrai, I had the wind right up.
We're turning now for home again, our hopes were unavailed
For there were twenty Halberstadts, a-sitting on my tail.

I went split-arse for glory, those buggers to avoid,
And when they saw such caperings, those Huns were overjoyed.
They emptied fifty pans or more, around my bloody head,
And they fired some high explosives and a ton or two of lead.

And now we've safely crossed the lines, and free at will to roam,
We're tickled up the crack and cannot find our home.
We land all over Western France, men everywhere they send
To work through all the ruddy night and dream of make and mend.

And now we're safely back again and feeling gay and bright
We'll take a car to Amiens and have dinner there tonight,
We'll stroll along the Boulevards, and meet the girls of France;
To hell with Army Medicos — we'll take our ruddy chance.

Additional verses:
Now, talking of Reconnaissance, I think you will agree,
That the best machine for this good work is hardly Number 3
For, although we do our best to please and earn the Major's thanks
For all the ruddy good we do, we may as well fly tanks.

Monday is the Guest night of Navy Number 3,
And last week we were very pleased to see the R.F.C.,
But when they introduced the game of old man Cardinal Puff,
They shortly got the Navy tight and things waxed bloody rough.

EVERYTHING.................. OVER CAMBRAI
(Parody on 'Everything is Peaches Down in Georgia')

Everything is splitarse over Cambrai,
What a peach of a height,
For a peach of a flight, believe me
There's a Fokker waiting up there for you,
Oh he's a peach of a Hun,
With a peach of a gun
Oh what a sod if he gets in the sun!
Mister Voss is bossing over Cambrai,
Always ready to shoot,
I bet he'll splitarse down at a hell of a rate
And you'll go home like an old Harry Tate!*
'Cause everything is splitarse over Cambrai.

**Harry Tate, the comedian, had his name appropriated in
rhyming slang with the R.E.8 aircraft.*

THINK OF ME

*An Observers' song to his Pilot to the tune 'Think of Me' from
the Musical Comedy, 'Yes, Uncle' demonstrating that things
have not changed in one respect in sixty-odd years.*

Think of me when your pressure's falling,
And you're almost stalling off the ground.
　　Think of me when your engine's stuttering,
　　And my heart is fluttering at the bloody sound.
Think of me when you crash on landing,
And your "Understanding" comes away,
Say you always think of me
For I'm thinking of you all day!

WHO KILLED COCK ROBIN?

Who killed Cock Robin?
    "I," said the Hun,
     "With my Lewis gun,
I killed Cock Robin."

CHORUS
All the planes in the air
Went a-dipping and a-throbbing,
When they heard of the death of poor Cock Robin,
When they heard of the death of poor Cock Robin.

Who saw him hit?
    "I." said old Fritz,
     "And I have a bit,
"I saw him hit."

CHORUS
Who saw him die?
    "I," said the spy,
     "With my telescopic eye,
I saw him die."

CHORUS

HURRAH FOR THE BOUNDING AIR

*A parody of the baritone song 'Hurrah for the Rolling Sea',
and remarkably akin in spirit to the later A25. It originated
with the R.N.A.S. who carried out patrols over the North
Sea and up to the Dutch Coast from R.N. Coastal Air Stations
such as Yarmouth, Felixstowe, and Killingholme.*

An aviator bold am I —
    Yo ho, my lads, Yo ho!
With joy I cleave the Eastern sky —
    Yo ho, my lads, Yo ho!
I love the roaring of the gale and hate the gentle breeze,
I hate a calm and placid day, but welcome storm-tossed seas.

Yo ho! Yo ho!
So let the tempest blow,
Hurrah, hurrah, for the atmosphere,
Hurrah for the bounding air.
With a Yo-heave-ho for the bumps that throw
You almost anywhere.
I saw a submarine one day,
I though it not quite safe to play,
So I dropped my bombs three miles away!
Hurrah for the bounding air.

Oh dud machines I always fly —
    Yo ho, my lads, Yo ho!
For then I know I can't get high —
    Yo ho, my lads, Yo ho!
For if I flew a new machine one day perhaps I'd meet
A Zeppelin or a Gotha, and for that I have cold feet.

Yo ho! Yo ho!
So let my bus be slow.
Hurrah, hurrah for the atmosphere,
Hurrah for the bounding air.
With a Yo-heave-ho for the bumps that throw
You almost anywhere.
On old BE's I hurl through space,
And hostile aeroplanes I chase,
But I know I haven't got their pace!
Hurrah for the bounding air.

I hate all forms of frightfulness —
    Yo ho, my lads, Yo ho!
I love the comfort of the Mess —
    Yo ho, my lads, Yo ho!
I love to sit in an easy chair before the blazing coal,
I much prefer my nice warm bed to the chilly Dawn Patrol.

Yo ho! Yo ho!
So let the others go.
Hurrah, hurrah for the atmosphere,
Hurrah for the bounding air,
With a Yo-heave-ho for the bumps that throw
You almost anywhere.
The honours list I read with zest,
I wish them all of luck, the best,
So long as I in peace can rest,
Hurrah for the bounding air!

STORMY THE NIGHT

Another parody, this time from the R.F.C., but popular in R.N.A.S.
messes, of the then renowned bass-baritone ballad "Asleep in the
Deep."

Stor my the night and a lowering sky,
 Proudly the plane doth ride.
List how the Observer's startled cry
 Rings as he clutches the side.
There in his cockpit the pilot lays,
 Cursing his ballast who weakly prays.
Though death be near, he knows no fear,
 For at his side are a dozen beer.

Chorus
 Brightly the flares from the landing ground blaze
 Bidding us list to the hint it conveys.
 Pilot take care – pilot take care!
 Hundreds have crashed, so beware, beware!
 Many brave hearts have neglected their charts,
 So beware, beware!

What of the tempest the following morn?
 There is no trace or sign,
Save where the wreckage bewstrews the corn
 Peacefully the sun doth shine.
But ere the wild raging storm did stop
 Two gallant airmen were caught on the hop,
No more to roam, afar from home,
 No more forced landings because of the Gnome*.
 Brightly the flares from the landing ground blaze,
 Bidding us list to the hint it conveys.
 Pilot take care, pilot take care!
 Hundreds have crashed so beware, beware!
 Many brave hearts have been mixed with spare parts,
 So beware, beware!

*Gnome rotary engine.

12

THE AIR CINDERELLAS

From 14 Squadron, R.N.A.S., a heavy bomber unit equipped with Handley Page 0/100's (One hundred feet wing span) mainly night bombing German targets in Belgium from their base at Coudekerque. Though Trenchard would probably have been loth to admit, they were one of the units from which Bomber Command eventually grew, being 214 Squadron R.A.F. by the end of the war.

We're flying by day, and we're flying by night,
We've harried the Hun, and have put him to flight.
Oh, I tell you Life's great to R.N.A.S. fellers,
Who, I hear it is said, are the Air Cinderellas!
In the grey of the dawn, in the black of the night,
'Planes heavy with bombs, till at length they are light;
For the trails left behind us are always the tellers,
When the stunting is done by the Air Cinderellas.

THE OLD NINE–A

The De Havilland 9A was supplied to bomber squadrons on the Western Front after the amalgamation in 1918 of the R.N.A.S. with the R.F.C. to form the R.A.F. One such unit was 205 Squadron, which originally was Naval Five, based at Coudekerque. The following is a nice parody based on "A Bachelor Gay" from "The Maid of the Mountains."

When you're flying the old Nine-A on a bumpy, windy day,
And your engine begins to splutter and you think you've lost your way,
Be careful to keep your head to wind if you want to reduce your glide,
And side-slip over a down-wind fence,
If you want to remain inside your field,
If you want to remain inside, you want to remain inside.

Chorus
At eighty-five you head her in so nicely, a glide you should not exceed,
At seventy-five you flatten out precisely, and still you've got lots of speed,
At sixty-five you pull the stick back gently and put her on the floor.
But at fifty you'll be stalling,
And you'll realise you're falling,
And you'll crash her as you've never crashed before.

THREE GERMAN OFFICERS CROSSED THE RHINE
(TUNE: Mademoiselle from Armentiers)

Three German officers crossed the Rhine, parlez-vous,
Three German officers crossed the Rhine, parlez-vous,
Three German officers crossed the Rhine,
To fuck the women and drink the wine,
Inky-pinky parlez-vous.

They came unto a wayside inn,
The cheeky buggers they walked right in.

O Landlord have you a daughter fair,
With lily white tits and golden hair?

My daughter Sir, is much too young
To be fucked about by a son of a gun.

(Falsetto) Oh, Father dear I'm not too young
For I've been screwed by the parson's son.

So up the stairs and into bed
They fucked till she was nearly dead.

And now she's come to London Town,
And you can have her for half a crown.

1918-1939

INTER WAR YEARS

ARGUS MARU
(TUNE: "Miralto Maree")

There once was an old Aircraft Carrier,
An exceedingly old Aircraft Carrier;
And she went by the name of the "Argus Maru"
        The Argus, the Argus, the Argus Maru

She went for a trip out to China,
An exceedingly fine trip to China.
And they landed some chaps on the racecourse
        From the Argus, the Argus, the Argus Maru.

And there they all set their hearts on
A Russian Princess from the "Carlton"
Who took all the cash from the Argus Maru
        The Argus, the Argus, the Argus Maru.

And then of course there was Ethel
And all her delectable crew,
Who took more cash from the Argus Maru
        The Argus, the Argus, the Argus Maru.

And now we are back at Gibraltar,
We're stuck in the dock at Gibraltar.
And there we shall booze for the rest of the cruise
        In the Argus, the Argus, the Argus Maru.

NOTE: The song obviously relates to the sojourn of
"Argus" in China during the "troubles", 1927.

BOMBING SONG
(TUNE: John Brown's Body)

The skies are filled with roaring, and unutterably bored
We're bogging round the Carrier with practice bombs on board,
Wasting time and petrol we can very ill afford,
But Heifer-dust boys, drive on!

CHORUS:
Glory! Glory Alleluia!
Glory! Glory Alleluia!
Glory! Glory Alleluia!
Yes, Heifer-dust, boys, drive on!

He hath trumpeted "Reconnaissance is tiresome and effete,
You need to practice neither that nor Spotting for the Fleet,
One-way-traffic-bombing is the very best of meat",
So Heifer-dust boys, drive on!

In a beautiful formation the Air Striking Force you'll see;
It ought to fill with jealousy poor wops like you and me,
Say not "upon our proper job we'd far prefer to be",
But Heifer-dust, boys, drive on!

So we're coming like the Glory of the Morning on the Wave,
With someone's best intentions half the halls of hell to pave,
Though in fact our war-load's sugar-all, what more could mortal crave?
So Heifer-dust, boys, drive on!

BLACKBURNS FLY OVER THE OCEAN
(TUNE: Bring Back my Bonnie to Me)

The Blackburns fly over the ocean,
The Blackburns fly over the sea,
If it wasn't for King George's Blackburns
Where the hell would the Fleet Air Arm be?

> CHORUS: *Heifer-dust, Heifer-dust!*
> *It's like heifer-dust to me, to me.*
> *Heifer-dust, Heifer dust!*
> *It's like heifer-dust to me, to me.*

The Darts are all stuck in the Hangar,
And the Flycatchers' engines aren't sound,
But the Blackburns are doing the business
While the bums are all stuck on the ground!

> CHORUS: *Heifer-dust, Heifer-dust! etc...*

Step into your aerial greenhouse
And force the old motor around,
And go for a trip in the ether,
And laugh at those frogs on the ground.

> CHORUS: *Heifer-dust, Heifer-dust! etc ...*

Single seaters are good for a roar up;
But they frequently park in the ditch,
While the Bisons commanded by Willums
Are all of them tickety-snitch.

> CHORUS: *Heifer-dust, Heifer-dust! etc ...*

The Blackburns fly over the ocean,
The Blackburns fly near and afar,
But do they land on again? — NEVER!
They always go back to Novar (Halfar).

NOTES:
The term "Heifer-dust" replaced a less polite word of two syllables. It subsequently became universal in the Fleet Air Arm as synonymous with "hot air".

WILLUMS, mentioned in verse 4 — T.M. Williams, R.A.F. — O.C. 423 (F.S.) Flight, 1927—29.

THE BICKER OF GREY
(TUNE: The Vicar of Bray)

In good Victoria's golden days
One thought it little harm meant,
That Fleets should strive in divers ways
To gain themselves preferment;
Their brass all shone, their guns all missed
The marks where they were pointed;
Still then one felt they could resist
All foes the Lord appointed.

> CHORUS: But this is the law, one will maintain,
> Until one's dying day, Sir
> Ho! down with the Navy, down the drain!
> One's Bumpf shall bicker and bray, Sir.

When Royal Edward claimed the Crown
It soon became the fashion,
In Stern Reality to drown
For polishing all passion.
Though this was hardly like to fit
The Navy's constitution,
Those simple Seadogs made of it
Another Evolution.

> CHORUS: But now this law, one will maintain
> Until one's dying day, Sir
> Ho! down with the Navy, down the drain
> One blithely'll blither away, Sir.

When George our King was then declared
In Aviation's grievance!
One first involved oneself, and sheared
From Admiral's allegiance;
All principles one did revoke,
Set logic at a distance,
What need a Navy to invoke
With heifer-dust for subsistence?

> CHORUS: So this is the law, one will maintain,
> Until one's dying day, Sir
> Ho! down with the Navy, down the drain!
> Let's sing, shout, print and pray, Sir.

When wicked William thought to clean
The slate of England's glory,
Once more enacted then was seen
The old and sordid story:
The Fleet remained within its base
(Silent in moderation),
Nor issued forth until had peace
Dispelled all provocation.

CHORUS: *So this is the law, one will maintain,*
    Until one's dying day, Sir
    Ho! down with the Navy, down the drain,
    Down, down and never cry "stay", Sir.

Though ne'er stalked hunger so before,
No U-Boats loomed so big, Sir
What purpose ships served in the War
One still can never twig, Sir;
Because all reason one's abjured
No fears need one engender,
Of thinking that the Fleet secured
This Island from surrender.

CHORUS: *Instead this law one will maintain*
    Until one's dying day,
    Ho! down with the Navy, down the drain!
    Such sooth let none gainsay, Sir.

Since then the war days are over,
And peace is in succession,
'Tis more than waste, we Nordics swear
Of Fleets to keep possession.
Why, while there's air (some hot) should we
With ships and sailors palter?
Adastral House shall rule the sea
And wind be our exalter!

CHORUS: *So this is the law one will maintain,*
    Until one's dying day, Sir
    Ho! down with the Navy, down the drain!
    The sun's out, let's make hay, Sir.

NOTE
C.G. Grey, Editor of "The Aeroplane" had his knife into the Navy for years, though he became less acrid later. His somewhat prosy style is reflected in the frequent "one's" in the song e.g. "One's dying day".

COO! WHAT A SILLY IDEA!

While flying one day in a "Short",
Doing W/T don't you know,
   With the aerial out about four hundred feet,
   The Pilot looked over and saw something neat,
So earthwards we started to go.
And when we had got pretty low
   He said to me — "Just wind the aerial in, put on all
              The brakes and then shove in the pin".

I said — "Coo What a silly idea!
     Coo What a silly idea!
It's already wound up with two kids in a pram,
A bathing machine, and a South Parade tram;
Wind the bally thing in? No, I'm damned if I can!
     Coo What a silly idea!"

Our "buzzer" is bright but not brilliant:
Say ten-words-per-min., more or less.
   Comrade Trewin said "You'll have to buzz at high speed,
   Twenty-two words per minute is what you will need,
And you'll certainly be in a mess
If you can't read code, cypher and press,
   And they never make press at less than eighteen
   Or about twenty-two; well you know what I mean".

I said — "Coo What a silly idea!
     Coo What a silly idea!
I might with an effort read twelve, it is true;
You can sit down and buzz yourself blue,
Bit I'm sugared if I'M going to read twenty-two!
     Coo What a silly idea!"

NOTE
A very old FAA song dating from early Lee days, by
M. Farquhar (original Naval Observer's Course).
Trewin (verse 2 line 3) was an instructor, at one time
an Assistant Paymaster RN, and flew as an observer
at Jutland.

EAGLE SONG

I'm the famous Dean, the Wandering Leader,
I wave-a da flag,
I make-a da cag.
Alone, I stand upon the flying deck-a.
Da hairs on my knees
Dey wave in da breeze.

CHORUS
For we all come from the Eagle,
And we "barker" every day
And although it is illegal
On the flying deck we stay.

I'm the fattest man in all the Eagle,
I sweat at da pores,
I keep-a da stores,
I used to be da backbone of da army,
I get-a too stout,
So dey chuck-a me out.

I'm da Coston Gun, da Senior Looker
I drink-a da wine,
I shoot-a da line.
I gather all the other Lookers round me,
We have-a da talk
Then we make-a da caulk.

I'm the famous Paymaster "Expenses".
I run-a da mess,
'Zob xciterimis'.
Da messman come to me, he say "ow signor",
No get-a da egg!
(He pull-a my leg).

I'm da Commandante of da Dart Flight,
I drop-a da fish,
Whenever you wish.
One day we had to land upon "Courageous"
Some people dey tink
We go for a drink.

I'm the rather portly Mellin Williams,
Blood pressure too high
I cannot think why.
Da Doc. he say "you got-a to stop-a da boozing"
We have-a da cag.
But I go on da Wag!

(By L.G.B. Robinson and Peter Slessor, 1929)
"Barker" named after Doctor Barker, a keen sunbather.

THE FIGHTER PILOT
(TUNE: The Minstrel Boy)

The fighter pilot to the ship has gone,
  On the Quarter-deck you'll find him.
His telescope beneath his arm,
  And his sword belt slung behind him.
He sees defaulters every day,
  And puts them in the rattle.
He always draws his flying pay,
  But he never never goes to battle!

NOTE
*Believed to have been written by Harry Barlow
(1929) of 402 (F.F.) Flight, at a time when
his Flight was retained onboard its carrier
during a Malta period, owing to insufficient
accommodation at Hal Far. The song was a
slightly ironical comment on the work they
did in these circumstances.*

405
(TUNE: College Days)

405.................405...................
See each one in his bus controlling
Looping, diving, spinning, rolling!
405.................405...................
Glad to see them when they stroll in
  RAH! RAH! SIZ BOOM BAH!

405.................405...................
They're the chaps who keep the mess alive!
On gin they thrive,
  Names we never can forget;
  Never met a tougher set.
Rare old, fair old, right old
  Tight old Boozy 405!

NOTE
405 was a famous Fighter Flight.

22

THE "FURIOUS" SONG
(TUNE: Lily of Laguna)

We're the "Furious"
And though we may look curious,
Here
We lie
At anchor all the day,
Waiting for a signal from the R.A.A.
We range up in aircraft
And then more aircraft
Ans still more aircraft,
And then we strike down in the evening;
There'll be NO FLYING FOR TO-DAY.

NOTE
Believed to have been written by Paul Slessor. Commemorates the 1932 Spring Cruise – the first occasion on which three Carriers were to work as a combined squadron under R.A.A. from Malta. As so often happened on Spring Cruises, the best of intentions on everyone's part were made nugatory by the weather, and a good deal of time was spent "ranging up" and "striking down".

The sun was shining on the sheds,
Shining with all his might,
He did his very best to make
Hal Far look smooth and bright —
And this was odd because there were
No aeroplanes in sight.

The Flights were working sulkily
Because they thought that one
Had got no business to be there
When it was half past one.
"It's very rude of them" they said
"To come and spoil the fun".

In 445 and 446
The tanks were dry as dry;
You could not see a cloud because
No cloud was in the sky.
No 'planes were flying overhead —
There were no 'planes to fly.

The Lookers and Telegraphists
Were walking close at hand,
They wept like anything to see
The broken engines stand.
"If they would only mend them soon"
They said, "It would be grand".

"If seven men with seven mauls
"Hit them for half a year,
"Do you suppose" one Looker said,
"That we'd get in the air?"
"I doubt it" said the Leading Tel,
And shed a bitter tear.

"O Pilots come and fly with us!"
One harassed Looker said.
"A pleasant flip, a wireless trip,
"Patrol on nine oh red,
"And we could do with three or four
"To swing outside the shed."

The Flight Commander looked at him
But never a word he said;
The Flight Commander winked his eye,
And shook his heavy head —
Meaning to say he did not choose
To leave his office shed.

But four young pilots hurried up
    All eager for the show;
They rushed around their aeroplanes
    And made the blighters go.
And this was odd, because it was
    Unusual, you know.

Four other pilots followed them,
    And yet another four;
And thick and fast they came at last,
    And more, and more, and more;
While L.A.C.'s collected clothes
    And goggles from the store.

The Lookers and Telegraphists
    Ran swiftly to and fro,
Collecting all their instruments
    And code books for the show,
And all the little Faireys stood
    And waited in a row.

"The time has come", the Lookers said
    "To play with many things,
"With shorts—and ships—and signal books—
    "And spotting rules—and things—
"And what the variation is—
    "And why the azimuth rings".

"But wait a bit", the Pilots cried,
    "Before we take the air;
"For some of us must try and mend
    "That undercarriage there".
"Oh hurry", said the Wireless King
    And groaned in deep despair.

"A navigation exercise
    "Is clearly what we need;
"Spotting and wind finding as well
    "Are very good indeed.
"Now if you're ready, gentlemen
    "Let us take off with speed".

"But not with us", the Pilots cried
    Turning a knob or two;
"After such kindness, that would be
    "A dismal thing to do".
"Steer 056" the Lookers said,
    "And air speed eighty two".

"It was so kind of you to come
    "And you are very nice",
The Leading Tel said nothing but
    "Oh peace at any price,
"I wish they were not quite so deaf
    "I've had to call them twice".

"It seems a shame", the Pilots said
    "To play us such a trick,
"And take us from our nice Hal Far —
    "Do take us back there quick".
The Leading Tel said nothing but
    "The call sign's TOC 8 VIC".

"I weep for you", one Looker said
    "I deeply sympathise".
With sobs and tears he sorted out
    Charts of the largest size.
Holding his watch and rangefinder
    Before his streaming eyes.

"Oh Pilots", said the Head Looker,
    "You've had a pleasant run
"Shall we be trotting home again?"
    But answers came there none —
And this was scarcely odd, because
    The Gosport Tube was bum.

IN OTHER WORDS

I had a sad accident some time ago.
        The story is sad but true:
I was out on patrol in a "Fairey IIID" —
        The same thing might happen to you —
We toddled along for an hour, all went well.
But then after that I'm sorry to tell:
        The vibration first excited my suspicion,
        And we quickly found that three big ends had run,
        The machine assumed a vertical position
        And the Pilot said he reckoned we were done,
        The wings came off, and both the floats departed;
        And the last thing I remember as she splashed,
        Was the poor old bus appeared to fall to pieces.
                In other words ....
                        We crashed.

26

NO BALLS AT ALL IF YOUR ENGINE CUTS OUT

CHORUS:
No balls at all, no balls at all,
If your engine cuts out, you'll have no balls at all.

In the year Anno Domini 1924,
In the Kingdom of Basra there started a war,
H.Q. got excited and sent for old Bert,
To pull operations right out of the dirt.

Now this bold bad rough pilot set out to bomb,
His bombs were O.K. but his tank was not full.
The A.G. behind the pilot did shout,
"You'll have no balls at all if your engine cuts out".

They were just over Soom when the engine cut out,
And over the intercom came an agonised shout,
"If you land at the East of the Basrian Pass,
You might as well stick the Lewis gun right up your arse."

They looked o'er the side and 'twas plain to see,
Sheik Abdul Mohammed and his men were at tea.
Lounging around midst the sand and the rocks,
Discussing Spring fashions and pruning their cocks.

They landed and ran like the chaff in the wind,
Leaving those Arabs just ten feet behind.
They knew they were in for some terrible shocks,
So they bashed out their bollocks on big spiky rocks.

St. Peter reclined in a fleecy white cloud,
The Orderly Archangel came flapping around.
He said to St. Peter "It's quite plain to me,
I have here a message which you ought to see.

"It's by W/T and it's marked with a P,
Addressed to St. Peter repeat Holy Three.
It's sender is Bert and the date is today,
It says there's an aircraft that's heading our way".

They came in to land at the dead of the night,
They laid out the flarepath, they set it alight.
They fired off Very lights Red, Green and White,
To show them the wind and which way to alight.

Now when they had landed they were full of good cheer,
St. Peter said, "Come in lads let's split the odd beer."
The pilot replied in a voice high and shrill,
"I thank you, St. Peter, I thank you, we will."

The moral of this story is quite plain to see,
Look after your petrol wherever you be.
If among the Turks or the Gurks you must land,
Be sure that your bollocks are off beforehand.

THE OBSERVER'S LAMENT
(TUNE: The Blue Hungarian Band)

Now the first time that I went up in a Wireless Aeroplane
    Lah-di dadi dadi dadi dah,
I called them in the carrier and I called them up in vain,
    Lah-di dadi dadi dadi dah.
I waggled the condenser and I twirled the A.T.I.
I thumped upon the ruddy key and gave them "I.M.I."
Was there ever an observer more unfortunate than I?
    Lah-di dadi dadi dadi dah.

We always get the "wind up" when we go up in the air,
    Lah-di dadi dadi dadi dah,
I couldn't get the signal through, so I sent it down en clair,
    Lah-di dadi dadi dadi dah.
The Wireless Operators all fell down in a fit;
They took that ruddy signal and they showed the Admiral it.
Now I've got to see the Captain and I'm fairly in the shit.
    Lah-di dadi dadi dadi dah.

Now the first time that I landed on Argus' flying deck
    Lah-di dadi dadi dadi dah,
I went into the palisades and nearly broke my neck,
    Lah-di dadi dadi dadi dah.
There was a great commotion; the Captain gave a shout;
At first I couldn't find out what the fuss was all about;
Then they said that we had landed while the "negative" was out,
    Lah-di dadi dadi dadi dah.

One day I went up spotting for the Battlecruiser Squad.
    Lah-di dadi dadi dadi dah,
The day was thick and foggy and I couldn't see a yard,
    Lah-di dadi dadi dadi dah.
I couldn't see the B.C.S. and they could not see me;
All *I* could see was several salvos falling in the sea.
And every time I made "SS" it should have been "GG",
    Lah-di dadi dadi dadi dah.

(An early Naval Observer song – about 1922.
M. Farquhar responsible for the last two verses.)

SING A SONG OF SIXPENCE

Sing a song of sixpence, "Digger's" going to fly;
    Watch him yank a seaplane, up into the sky !
Watch the Drogue Observer burning-out-the-brake !
    Oh what a handsome couple those two cobbers make !

NOTE
"Digger" Dagg, R.A.F. — a famous F.A.A. character about
1922 – 1927.

THE SENIOR OBSERVER'S LAMENT

Maybe he's bombing, maybe he's spotting, maybe he's flying low.
Flew off this morning, when day was dawning, such a long time ago.
    I don't know where he is, or what made him go.
    One thing I know —
    I'm getting mighty worried !
Maybe he's lonesome, all on his ownsome, searching for who knows what.
Maybe he's boating, maybe he's floating, and again maybe not !
    I don't care what he steered, what wind he used, or why he left,
    So long as he'll only make his call-sign to me !

(By W.T. Couchman)

29

AND WHEN THE BALL WAS OVER– THERE WERE FOUR AND TWENTY LESS...
RPC
1215–

1939-45

THERE'S A HOME FOR BATCHY AIRMEN
(TUNE: There's a Home for Little Children)

There's a home for batchy airmen
'Way out in the sunny Sudan
The airmen are all batchy
And so is the fucking Old Man.
There's bags and bags of bullshit
Saluting on the square,
And when we're not saluting
We're up in the fucking air.

Now two long years I've been here
Among the shit and sand,
The sun has burned my eyeballs
The sun has scorched my hand.
We're flying in the sunshine,
Saluting in the rain
And when we go from Khartoum
We'll never come back again.

We're leaving Khartoum in the cattle saloon
We're sailing by night and by day,
We've passed Kasfareet, we've got fuck-all to eat
'Cause we've given our rations away.

So shine, shine, 'Somersetshire'
The skipper looks on her with pride.
He'd have a blue fit if he saw anyshit
On the side of the 'Somersetshire'.

This is my story,
This is my song.
I've been in the Navy
Too fucking long.
So roll out the "Nelson", the "Rodney", "Renown",
You can't have the "Hood" 'cause the bastard's gone down.

AIR SEA RESCUE
(TUNE: The Church's One Foundation)

We are the Air Sea Rescue,
No ruddy use are we,
The only time you'll see us
Is breakfast, lunch or tea.
And if you're in the 'oggin
By day or in the night,
Per ardua ad Astra
Fuck you Jack I'm all right.

YOU'LL NEVER GO TO HEAVEN

Now you can't go to heaven on roller skates,
'Cos you'll roll right past — those pearly gates (repeat)

CHORUS:
I ain't going to grieve my Lord no more.

Oh you'll never go to heaven in a Seafire three,
Because a Seafire three don't go to sea.

Oh you'll never go to heaven in a Firefly,
Because a Firefly can't fly that high.

Oh you'll never go to heaven in a F.6.F.
Because an F.6.F. has no V.H.F.

Oh you'll never go to heaven in a chevrolet
Because a Chevrolet don't know the way.

Oh you'll never go to heaven with a bottle of gin,
Because St. Peter won't let you in.

Oh you'll never go to heaven in a woman's arms,
Because the Lord don't hold with feminine charms.

Oh you'll never go to heaven in powder and paint,
Because the Lord don't love you as you ain't.

Oh you'll never go to heaven in a Barra two,
Because the wings arrive before you do.

Oh you'll never go to heaven in a Tiger Moth,
Because a Tiger Moth is built of cloth.

Oh you'll never go to heaven in a Vought Corsair,
Because a Vought Corsair won't get you there.

Oh you'll never go to heaven in a Ford Coupe,
Because the Lord has shares in Chevrolet.

Oh you'll never go to heaven in a Firebrand,
Because the Firebrand sticks close to land.

Oh you'll never go to heaven with an A.E.O.
Because the A.E.O.s go down below.

Oh you'll never go to heaven in an Albacore,
Because an Albacore has prangs galore.

Oh you'll never go to heaven in a Buccaneer,
Because a Buccaneer's too hard to steer.

Oh you'll never go to heaven in a Seaking,
Because the Seaking's an unnatural thing.

Oh you'll never go to heaven if your wings don't fold,
'Cos you won't get them through those gates of gold.

Oh you'll never go to heaven if the weather's wet,
'Cos the Lord ain't got no beacons yet.

If you get to heaven before I do,
Just drill a hole and pull me through.

THEY SAY THERE'S A (............) JUST LEAVING

The original version belonged to the R.N.A.S., but later this sensationally popular ditty became very much taken over by the R.A.F.

They say there's a flat top just leaving .... bound for old Blighty's shore,
Heavily laden with terrified men shit scared and flat on the floor.
They say there are Messerschmitts pumping in lead, they say there 190s too,
They shot off our bollicks and fucked the hydraulics so cheer up my lads fuck 'em all.

CHORUS:
Fuck 'em all, fuck 'em all, the long and the short and the tall,
Fuck all the sergeants and W.O.1s, fuck all the corporals and their bastard sons.
For we're saying goodbye to them all as up the C.O.'s arse they crawl,
You'll get no promotion this side of the ocean, so cheer up my lads fuck 'em all.

With six Q.D.Ms. and some fucking good luck we get back to .... shore,
The cloud was 11/10ths right on the deck, in fact 'twas a fucking sight more.
In ten fucking years when they're digging for coal in a bloody great hole close to Wick,
They'll dig up a .... two beds and a shitehawk, so cheer up my lads fuck 'em all.

The other poor bastards who fell in the shit, they sent them to ....
The runway was 90 deg. out of wind it tried fucking hard to be more.
Now Coastal Command think this is fucking good fun, they chortle like bastards and say
"We'll get our promotion this side of the ocean if 899 fly every day."

These fucking controllers are driving me mad, they don't know a map from a chart,
They think that a shitbag's a bag full of shit, a wind lane the track of a fart,
They think that a Sextant's a man of the church, a bearing a little steel ball,
We talk about bombsights they think we're three parts tight, 'cos a bombsight's got no
                                                                                    eyes at all.

BALLS-UP
(TUNE: "The Hut Sat Song")

CHORUS: *There's a balls up on the flight deck*
And the Wavy Navy done it,
There's a balls up on the gangway
And they don't know who to blame.

The K.G.V.'s ten miles astern,
She should be ten ahead
Cos every turn the carrier made
Was blue instead of red.

> Twelve Albacores were neatly ranged
> To bomb and blitz Bordeaux
> Commander "F" was sold a pup
> 'Cos seven wouldn't go.

The Captain's walk was disturbed by the talk
Of the fishermen on the rail
A-talking dirt and swopping skirt
From Hatston, Twatt and Crail.

> There's 'reds' galore from an Albacore
> Hell-diving for the drink
> Di-dah di-dah comes from afar
> As a Fulmar starts to sink.

A solitary straight "A" watched,
As the first one hit the barrier.
"My god! these H.O.'s may wear wings,
But they're fuck all use in a carrier".

After the A25, a very popular 'Branch' war-time song,
reflecting the enomous preponderance of RNVR personnel
over RN. There are many slight variations in the words,
and, as with the A25 it has been impossible to print an
'exact' varsion.

FLYING FLYING FORTRESSES
(TUNE: John Brown's Body)

We're flying Flying Fortresses at forty thousand feet,
Flying over Germany to give the Huns a treat,
We've bags and bags of ammo, and a teeny weeny bomb
And we drop the bastard from so high we don't know where it's gone.

CHORUS
We were only flying Fortresses,
We were only flying Fortresses,
We were only flying Fortresses,
And we drop the bastard from so high we don't know where it's gone.

We're flying Fairey Swordfish at fifty fucking feet,
Through hail and rain and snow and through the fucking sleet,
And when we think we're flying south, we find we're flying north
And we make our fucking landfall in the Firth of fucking Forth.

CHORUS
We were only flying Swordfish, etc..
And we make our fucking landfall in the Firth of fucking Forth.

We're flying little Seafires and we're flying straight along
Though the petrol's mighty short, the briefing's mighty long.
We've bags and bags of briefing and a teeny spot of gas
And we never see the 109 that comes right up our arse.

CHORUS
We were only flying Seafires, etc..
And we never see the 109 that comes right up our arse.

We're flying Barracudas and we're getting bags of twitch,
We sit up there and think about the time we'll have to ditch,
Our job's to find the enemy and sink him with a fish,
But to get back home to England is our only fucking wish.

CHORUS
We were only flying Barras, etc.
And to get back home to England is our only fucking wish.

We're flying Fairey Fireflies, forcing off from Abbotsinch
Through a haze from Glasgow where ye canna see an inch
Roon an' roon the Trossachs, and doon the Ayrshire coast
We are the Wavy Navy is our proudest fucking boast.

CHORUS
We were only flying Fireflies, etc.....
And we are the Wavy Navy is our proudest fucking boast.
(With acknowledgements to 1830 R.N.V.R. Squadron)

We're flying Hawker Furies from the "Glory" all day long,
Flying in to Paengyong-do, then up to Chaeryong.
Sometimes we go further north and think we are big
But it's flat on the deck and out to sea if ever we hear a Mig.

CHORUS
We were only flying Furies, etc..
And we're flat on the deck and out to sea if ever we hear a Mig.

We flew the North Atlantic till it made us fucking weep,
The sea was fucking cold and wet and very fucking deep,
The Ops. room up at Lossie is simply fucking rotten,
And Lossie will stay here till we're fucking well forgotten.

We joined this fucking Navy 'cos we thought it fucking right,
We don't care if we fly or if we fucking fight,
But what we do object to are those fucking Ops. room twats,
Who sit there sewing rings on at the rate of fucking knots.

And when this war is over and we leave the fucking branch,
The regulars will still be in and won't we fucking laugh,
We'll be yachting in the Isle of Wight, shooting in the North,
While whose bastards make their landfalls in the Firth of fucking Forth.

**Another very popular 'number' with many variations of text, and one
which stretched beyond the technical limits of this section − like
'You'll Never Go to Heaven'.*

THE STRINGBAG SONG
(TUNE: My Bonnie Lies over the Ocean)

My Stringbag flies over the ocean,
My Stringbag flies over the sea,
If it wasn't for King George's Swordfish,
Where the hell would the Royal Navy be ?

CHORUS:
Stringbag, Stringbag,
Oh, bring back my Stringbag to me, to me,
Stringbag, Stringbag,
Oh, bring back my Stringbag to me.

At Taranto and chase of the Bismark,
In the battle of Cape Matapan,
'Twas the fish from the Swordfish that fixed 'em,
And those who could run, how they ran !

Now the science of dropping torpedoes
Is taught at R.N.A.S. Crail,
Where the instruction's so good that pupils
With the Swordfish aren't likely to fail.

No doubt when we get Barracudas.
The Swordfish's day will be done,
So remember, 'twas this kite that fixed 'em,
And gave them their place in the sun !

THESE SHAKY DO'S

(TUNE: These Foolish Things)

That ropey batsman's signals Oh, so vague;
Those long approaches over Ailsa Craig;
The sight of many a wreck,
A prang on the deck,
Remind me of FOO.

That Babs that didn't work, that u/s Rooster,
The sight of Harvey going off the booster,
the stolid look of Wings —
These foolish things,
Remind me of FOO.

Biggest Boat yet afloat,
You frighten me;
My lifebelt's in my hand
Whenever we're out of sight of land.
Those evening sessions when we all got plastered,
Those evening sessions when we all got plastered,
And drank a toast to Britain's biggest bastard;
Nine Wing* is still on the booze —
These shaky do's,
Remind me of FOO.

Lt. Aldcroft.
9 Wing comprised 820 – 826 Squadrons HMS Indefatigable.

THANKS FOR THE MEMORY

Thanks for the memory,
Of biplanes in the sky,
Of pilots who could fly,
Of four hour trips, attacking ships,
Returning with a sigh,
How lovely it was.

Thanks for the memory,
Of large fixed undercarts
Of Hatston playing darts,
Of Buster rushing round to fix
Old Digger for spare parts,
How lovely it was.

Many's the time we've pranged 'em
On many a A.L.T.
Many's the time we've slanged 'em,
No A.S.V.! No W/T!

So thanks for the memory,
Of only one front gun,
With which to hack the Huns
Of dripping oil and hangar toil,
And gen that weighed a ton,
How lovely it was.

Thanks for the memory,
Of pitching decks at night,
Observers full of fright,
Of taking off with little wind,
And dropping out of sight,
How lovely it was.

We said goodbye to the carrier,
We gave all our aircraft away,
And now we've no fear of the barrier,
For here we stay for many a day.

So thanks for the memory,
Of drunken nights ashore,
Of blacks put up galore,
Of gin and limes and flying times,
And popsies by the score,
How lovely it was.

N.B. Alternate names in verse 2 are
Helston, Willis and Uncle Sam.

I JUST GOT ANOTHER WAVE-OFF
(TUNE: John Brown's Body)

He gave me a 'Low Dip' and a 'Roger' in the groove,
I have had a 'High' and 'Fast', but what's it going to prove?
The L.S.O. will kill you yet, but what're you going to do
"I'll make that bastard jump into the net."

CHORUS
I just got another wave-off,
I just got another wave-off,
I just got another wave-off
But I made that bastard jump into the net.

If the ship is on my wing he says I'm close it seems,
So if I move a foot more out then I'm far too wide abeam.
If he waves me off again I'm ready and I'm set
I'll make that bastard jump into the net.

YOU WORK THE W/T
(TUNE: Loch Lomond)

You work the W/T, and I'll work the R/T,
And we might get a T.O. between us,
But I think the best thing is for you to raise a stand,
And semaphore the time with your penis.

HARRY CLAMPERS
(TUNE: Johnny Pedlar)

Each morning on the dot
If you want fog, I got;
And if you're still half-pissed,
A leetle Scotch mist;
Mornings after you've all been to town,
Harry Clampers never lets you down.

And if the Flight Deck party
Hasn't pranged your wings or props
I got low cloud — Make you think
I'm still the tops!

And if you really need
To crash your filthy swede,
Then just ignore the Met,
I got the best Met yet;
I shall deepen Schoolie's worried frown —
Harry Clampers never lets you down.

SWEET FA
(TUNE: Sweet Fanny Adams)

We used to do bags of navexes,
But now that they've thrown them away,
While pranging the Tirpitz the TAG and Observer
Do sweet F.A.

CHORUS
Sweet Fanny Adams, sweet F.A! While pranging..etc.

We used to dive down at two-eighty,
But now we have come to D-Day
What we do less than a good round four hundred
Is sweet F.A!

CHORUS
Sweet Fanny Adams, sweet F.A! What we do less...etc.

We've low-flown all over the 'oggin,
Now we'll low-fly all over Norway;
Till all that is left of the paint on our Barras
Is sweet F.A!

CHORUS
Sweet Fanny Adams, sweet F.A! Till all that .....etc.

I was sitting one day on the booster,
And the Plumbers were anxious to play;
Came a WHOOSH and a clatter — and there I was sitting
On sweet F.A!

CHORUS
Sweet Fanny Adams, sweet F.A! Came a WHOOSH.....etc.

I was coming in one day to land her,
But the batsman got right in the way;
Now all that is left of his bats and his bollocks
Is sweet F.A.!

CHORUS
Sweet Fanny Adams, sweet F.A! Now all that is left.... etc.

We were diving balls-out in a gaggle,
When the Wing Leader got in the way;
The wings, props and tailplanes fell slowly to earth
Leaving sweet F.A!

CHORUS
Sweet Fanny Adams, sweet F.A! The wings, props... etc.

S/Lt. J.F.F.Callear

832 SQUADRON SONG*
(TUNE: "Take Me Back To Dear Old Blighty")

Take me back to Navy Norfolk,
Put me on the bus for B.O.Q.**
Put me in the bogs,
In among the wogs,
Reading all about V.D. there's fuckall else to do.

You won't get a fucking cabin,
You'll be put in Dormitory 'A'.
Oh isn't it fucking awful,
Living in Navy Norfolk,
The arsehold of the U.S.A.

*Composed in 1943 just after 832 Sqn. had worked up
on Avengers at Norfolk, Virginia, and were on their
way to Hawaii in HMS *Victorious.*

** Bachelor Officers' Quarters.

811 SQUADRON SONG*
(TUNE: "Road to the Isles)

There's a squadron going rotten, for it's waiting for the war
    And the war is waiting for the Adm'reltee.
Eight eleven's simply heaven if you want to stay ashore,
    For we ne'er, never, ever go to sea.

CHORUS
From Lee-on-Solent to Arbroath and Machrihanish you may pass;
    You may search the bars and brothels far and wide;
For we've flown until we've grown a pair of wings upon our arse
    But we'll never see the Biter in the Clyde.

We've been doing Army Co-op during morning, noon and night,
    Shooting up the ruddy pongoes far and wide;
Diving down upon the Brown jobs from a ruddy enormous height
    Starts a spot of twitching in the old back-side!

*Composed some time during the twelve-month period before 811
eventually "saw the *Biter* in the Clyde" in March 1943. There
were many other verses, all, alas, forgotten after 811 and 812
Sqns. were amalgamated in December 1942.

THE PREGNANT SWORDFISH*
(TUNE: "She was poor but she was Honest")

Oh, I used to think my Swordfish
    Was as slow as she was tame,
But I'm sorry to inform you
    She has lost her maiden name.

For she's going to have a baby;
    You can see that by the shape.
You can tell from her performance
    She's been sub-jected to rape!

See that bloody great protrusion?
    You can spot it from afar.
If you ask me what's inside it —
    It's a bastard like its ma!

Once my thoroughbred old Swordfish
    Was my pride and my delight,
But I've had her now she's preggers;
    I'll go fly some other kite.

*In January, 1944, 811 Sqn. were re-equipped with
Swordfish Mark III, fitted with the Mk.XI radar,
with bulbous scanner under the fuselage.*

THE FLYING FORTY-SECOND — 742*

Come listen to my story
Of a Squadron bold and strong,
Whose deeds are worth recordin'
In poetry and song.
'Twas formed for special duty
So let's give them their due;
They're in a spin
With fingers in —
It's Seven Forty Two.

CHORUS BETWEEN VERSES

*Oh, the flying forty-Second,
Old seven forty-two;
Come join us friend,
Go round the bend
With seven forty-two.*

43

The monsoon's just a-breakin'
Dark clouds are in the sky.
"Get Coimbatore"
"The ruddy bore
Won't answer" is the cry!
The wireless it's a shocker
The T.A.G. is chokker
There ain't no hope,
You've just Joe Soap
In Seven Forty Two.

The pilots of the aircraft,
The captains of the sky,
They have no art
With map or chart
And they can barely fly.
They mount into the cockpit,
And scramble through the blue,
And lose their way
Most every day
In Seven Forty Two.

The T.A.G.'S, the wireless men —
A silly lot of clots —
They haven't got a clue
Which are the dashes or the dots,
They cannot work the wireless,
We don't know what they do —
Bar get the Forces Programme
For Seven Forty Two.

Then we have the ground crew,
Who service the machine;
The engine's dud,
It's full of mud
They cannot keep it clean,
The E.O.'s got no gumption,
We've never known him function;
There's no one who
Has got a clue
In Seven Forty Two.

The Squadron you'll have gathered
Is Seven Forty Two;
We'll fly you here,
We'll fly you there,
And always get you through.
We fly o'er desert spaces,
O'er green and fertile places
O'er land and sea and through the blue,
That's Seven Forty Two.

Last Chorus

Oh, the Flying Forty Second,
Old Seven Forty Two;
In spite of all,
We're on the ball,
In Seven! In Seven!! in SEVEN FORTY TWO!!!

**742 Squadron was re-organised into an R.N. Air
Transport Squadron, equipped with Beechcraft
Expediters to operate from Southern India on
1 November 1944. From Sulur (Coimbatore) they
had regular scheduled services to Cochin, Colombo,
Trincomalee, Bangalore and Madras. The song is
one of many from a bound volume and composed
by the C.O., the late Lt. Cdr. Neville Stack.*

DUAL CONTROL

Oh come with me my lady and together let us fly,
And I will teach you all I know when we are in the sky,
Though the Harvard may be grisly I will try and make it do,
When I have a spot of dual control with you.

You'll learn exactly how (and what) to take off and perhaps,
You'll not feel too embarassed when lowering your flaps,
There is one way up the runway I am anxious to pursue,
When I have a spot of dual control with you.

But when you're warmed up properly you'll realize the thrills,
Of lifting up your undercart and opening your gills,
You'll be purring to the whirring of my variable screw,
When I have a spot of dual control with you.

If when I flash my weapon you should do a barrel roll,
With the joystick in your cockpit you must exercise control,
For to get your carburettor flooded out would never do,
When I have a spot of dual control with you.

But if you think that all is lost then do not be a dunce,
Just call on Doctor Homer to prescribe for you at once,
So be clever dear and never let yourself get overdue,
When I have a spot of dual control with you.

NIGHT WATCH
Tribute to the W.R.N.S. R.P. Branch
Tune:— 'Lullaby of Broadway

She sits there knitting by the fire,
　With down bent head, nor seems to tire;
She sits there knitting hour by hour,
　All by herself in her lonely tower.

Outside the moon has bared her face,
　The evening mists creep on apace,
Up in the radiance of the night
　There sits another trained to fight.

Up and down his moonlit beat
　He watches all from his lonely seat,
Soon he hears his Station calling—
　'Bandit approaching' in their warning.

He's vectored, left, he's vectored right,
　The bandit soon should be in sight,
And then ahead, as sure as fate,
　There looms a prowling Eighty-Eight.

'Tally-ho-the chase is on,
　Heedless now of where he's gone,
O'er vale and meadow, hill and lea
　He chases his quarry out to sea.

Now at last he opens fire—
　One fatal burst, a flaming pyre—
His work is done, — he looks around
　To find a pinpoint on the ground.

Alas, no terra-firma there,
　But water, water everywhere.
The moon has flown, the night is black
　'Oh Jesus, Twinkle, get me back'.

And sure enough her voice rings out—
　'O.K. — orbit and turn about'.
He hopes to Heaven she's got a clue
　And knows what she's been taught to do.

Fearful still he longs to hear
　The homeward course that he must steer
Fearful 'cos his fuel is low,
　Fearful of the sea below.

Hours it seems before his prayer
Is answered as he circles there,
Granting him new lease of life...
'Seaweed calling — steer two one fife'.

Eagerly he turns for home,
Turns towards his aerodrome,
Straining downwards through the dark
Trying to pick up some landmark.

But he finds to his dismay
Clouds and rainstorms bar his way,
Leaving him no other choice
Than to trust that silvery voice.

'Orbit now, you're over base'.
And there below he sees the place.
With heartfelt thanks his leave he takes—
'Goodnight' she says as he pancakes.

And still she sits there, hour by hour
Throughout the night, nor seems to tire;
She does her work unfailingly,
God bless Twinkle — CERTAINLY'

written by: Lt. Jimmy Hancock OX DICO
HMS Pretoria Castle

893 SQUADRON SONG

circa 1943. Equipment — Martlets.
SHIP: H.M.S. Formidable. C.O. — Lt. Cdr. Pearson

WE ARE SQUADRON NUMBER EIGHT-NINE-THREE
AND PRETTY BLOODY SOON THEY'RE GOING TO SEND US OFF TO SEA;
THEY TELL US THAT WE'VE GOT TO LEARN TO FLY AND FIGHT AND SHOOT...
BUT THEY CAN STICK THEIR BLOODY FIGHTING UP THEIR OWN SHIT-CHUTE!

WHEN THEY SEE US THEY'LL BEGIN TO SHOUT
"IT'S TIME THIS BLOODY SQUADRON PULLED THEIR FINGERS OUT! "
(Slowly, with feeling)
WE'RE THE FLYING BOYS WHO NEVER WANT TO GO TO SEA...
CLEAR THE PORTSIDE OF THE FLIGHT DECK ....

(lente, pianissimo) .... FOR EIGHT-NINE-FOO -OO-EEEE
/building to................ off-key CRESCENDO')

Copyright: Malcolm McPhee and other bograts of 893

WYKEHAM HALL
(Tune: Bless'Em All)

Wykeham Hall, Wykeham Hall,
The Captains, the Subs, take 'em all.
Bull is their motto, they'll have it or bust,
Their carpets are knee deep in pure heifer dust.
They think that they're a hell of a crew,
But between them they ain't got a clue,
But that does not matter
They sit down and natter
With fingers well in
WYk-Em-All

A PILOT'S LOT

*Parody of 'A Policeman's Lot' from
'The Pirates of Penzance'*

When a Pilot's not impinging on the barrier (on the barrier)
Or trying his unwilling crew to drown (crew to drown)
If you cannot find him drinking in the wardroom of the carrier
It's safe to bet his head he's crashing down (crashing down)
While he's waiting apprehensive on the booster (on the booster)
And Commander (Flying) takes his bloody time (bloody time)
When he's trying to home his aircraft on the rooster (on the rooster)
Then the pilot sits and thinks "Gaw" what a gime ("Gaw" what a gime)
When there's taxi-driving duties to be done (to be done)
Then a pilot's lot is not a happy one (happy one)

An Observer's handicapped by major space considerations
Unless by chance he should be very small (very small)
Beacon sets and several other installations (installations)
It's a wonder he can operate at all (-ate at all)
When the poor old "O" comes staggering down the flight deck like a porter,
With canvas sack and chartboard in his hand (in his hand)
His parachute he wears because they tell him he oughter
Hanging round his legs so that he can hardly stand (hardly stand)
When there's back seat jobs and plotting to be done (to be done)
An Observer's lot is not a happy one (happy one).

THE MODERN METEOROLOGIST

*Parody of 'The Modern Major General' from
'The Pirates of Penzance'*

I am the very model of a modern Meteorologist,
A scientific calling and one needing no apologist,
I diagnose the weather without any doubt or lingerin' —
The forecast turns out well on days I haven't got my finger in.
I'm pally with St. Swithin and Old Moore's an ancient friend of mine,
J. Pluvius, the weather clerk, and Buchan often send a line,
And if it's necessary I'm delighted to inspire a
Correspondence with the shades of Ananias and Sapphira.
I explain my charts to callers in a useful terminology —
Of words that might mean anything, of doubtful etymology;
Houdini isn't in it, I'm that noted escapologist,
That equivocating casuist, the modern Meteorologist.
I keep the pilots well supplied with 'gen.' on visibility,
The customers are satisfied, our motto is civility.
I tell them what the weather's like from Yeovilton to Stornoway,
And answer silly questions till the telephone gets worn away.
To please the Plotting Office Wren I read the anemometer,
And give her information, though I'd rather throw a bomb at her;
But the duty I like best of all my duties is the daily 'un —
Explaining things away with learned words sesquipedalian,
For when I get involved in conversation catechitical,
I obfuscate the questioner with answers most political.
The science does not matter, I'm a skilful escapologist
Who'll get away with anything, a modern Meteorologist.
In fact when I know what is meant by equigeopotential,
When I can speak to brass-hats in a manner consequential,
When I have learnt to change a simple statement to a paragraph,
And tell unhesitatingly a wind-vane from a barograph;
When I can make Commander (F) believe my forecasts fictional
And carefully constructed with the help of rules predictional,
When I've become a walking encyclopaedia of weather lore, —
I'll qualify to occupy that office on the nether floor,
When I can make a forecast read in terms still MORE ambiguous,
And base emphatic statements in synoptics quite exiguous,
Then I'll consider I've become that brilliant escapologist,
The pilots' guide and counsellor, the modern Meteorologist.

IF

With apologies to Rudyard Kipling.

If you can keep your track when all about you
Are losing theirs and setting "Mag" from "True";
If you can trust yourself when pilots doubt you
And get back to the ship out of the blue;
If you can keep control of your dividers
And Bigsworth board and Gosport tube and pad;
Or listen to the wireless and pilot
Talking in unison — and not go mad;

If you can bomb, and "Red on red" can master
If you can check the drift — and still take aim
If you can fire your gun and simply plaster
The target while you're spinning just the same;
If you can bear the cold and noise and slipstream;
If you can think — and not attempt to "zizz";
If you can make that fatuous code book seem
A little bit more useful than it is;

If you can do a swing and when correcting
Apply the magnet right way round and then
By patient, high endeavour and collecting
The data — make it simple for all men;
If you can take a sight — nor lose the bubble,
Or range — and use the proper height of haze,
Or take a fix — and not get into trouble
By putting deviations on both ways;

If you can spot, and not fall for the error
Of substituting "SS" for "GG";
If you can work the drogue, that holy terror,
And never let it fall into the sea;
If you can sight a fleet without detection,
Giving the right position to a dot;
If you can cope with every situation
And apply "immediate action" on the spot;

If you can keep your temper with the wireless,
Or shift your wave — nor lose the common touch;
If you can stop yourself becoming useless
By using too few clothes, or else too much;
If you can fill the unforgiving minute
With sixty seconds' worth of ground-speed run,
Yours is the Air — and everything that's in it,
And — which is more — you'll be an (O), my son.

N. de G. Weymouth

MR. PUPIL AND MR. INSTRUCTOR
(TUNE: Mr. Mercer and Mr. Crosby)

Oh, Mr. Instructor — Oh, Mr. Instructor,
Can you tell me how my flying's been assessed?
Though I spin out of control,
When I try a half flick roll,
A guy can do no better than his best.

Oh, Mr. Pupil — Oh, Mr. Pupil,
Say, your best is not quite good enough for me.
You'll enjoy much better health
In a thing that rolls itself.
        In a Martlet, Mr. Instructor?
        In a corvette, Mr. P.

Oh, Mr. Insturctor, Oh Mr. Instructor
All the other boys are hogging it today,
And I wanted to find out
What the noise is all about,
Are these Harvard aircraft really here to stay?

Oh Mr. Pupil. Yes, Mr. Instructor?
Though you other boys had Harts taped to a "Tee";
In the skyways you will play
In this same abandoned way
Straight and level Mr. Instructor?
Upward Charlies, Mr. P.

Oh Mr. Instructor, Yes, Mr. Pupil?
I've been reading in the flying magazines
When an aircraft starts to spin
Auto-rotation will set in
Can you tell me what this language really means?

Oh Mr. Pupil. Yes, Mr. Instructor?
When your aircraft speed begins to dwindle rapidly
If that aircraft starts to yaw
You're going to wind up on the floor
How too, too thrilling, Mr. Instructor
It's devastating Mr. P.

Oh Mr. Instructor. Yes, Mr. Pupil?
The man who teaches airmanship tells me
That the centrifugal force
Is enough to kill a horse
If you fool around at more than seven "G".

Oh Mr. Pupil. Yes, Mr. Instructor?
Once a guy who thought he knew a thing or three
Pulled the stick back at full power
At three hundred miles an hour
Did he get his wings Mr. Instructor?
On his shoulders, Mr. P.

Oh Mr. Instructor. Yes, Mr. Pupil?
These precautionary landings are a bore.
Now I'm holding off at last,
Only three feet from the grass,
Can you tell me what that horn is sounding for?

Oh Mr. Pupil, oh Mr. Pupil,
There's a handle on the left side don't you see.
If that handle's not pressed down,
You'll land too close to the ground,
A three-pointer, Mr. Instructor?
On your belly, Mr. P.

Oh Mr. Instructor. Yes, Mr. Pupil?
Is it true that flying's ancient as the hills
And the first galoot who flew
Way up in the skies so blue
Thought that 50 M.P.H. was packed with thrills?

Oh Mr. Pupil, oh Mr. Pupil,
Nowadays we have our airscrews made V.P.
With a boost of forty eight
When the throttle's through the gate
That's going places Mr. Instructor,
Mr. P. you're telling me.

Oh Mr. Instructor. Yes, Mr. Pupil?
It's a thousand pounds a U-boat they tell me,
When you see that U-boat's wake,
Why it's just a piece of cake.

You just drop your bombs and bog off home for tea.

Oh Mr. Pupil, oh Mr. Pupil,
A Marine dive-bombed a U-boat out at sea,
He did three-oh-nine straight down
In five minutes he came round.
In the water, Mr. Instructor?
In the U-boat, Mr. P.

TEN NEW SEAFIRES
(TUNE: Ten Green Bottles)

Ten new Seafires landing on the deck (repeat)
And if one Seafire pilot should break his fucking neck,
There'll be nine new Seafires landing on the deck.

Nine new Seafires landing on a carrier (r)
But if one new Seafire should hit the fucking barrier,
There'll be eight new Seafires landing on the carrier.

Eight new Seafires climbing higher and higher (r)
And if one new Seafire should miss the bloody wire,
There'll be seven new Seafires flying higher and higher.

Seven new Seafires flying now I think, (r)
And if one new Seafire should hit the bloody drink,
There'll be six new Seafires flying now I think.

Six new Seafires flying in formation, (r)
And if a pilot's weak through over fornication,
There'll be five new Seafires flying in formation.

Five new Seafires flying on a stunt, (r)
And if one Seafire pilot should act the bloody cunt,
There'll be four new Seafires flying on a stunt.

Four new Seafires flying round about, (r)
And if one Seafire pilot doesn't keep his finger out,
There'll be three new Seafires flying round about.

Three new Seafires, one piloted by Sal, (r)
And if Sal keeps thinking about his fucking moll,
There'll be two new Seafires neither piloted by Sal.

Two new Seafires one piloted by Tim. (r)
And if he keeps drinking that bloody awful Gin,
There'll be one new Seafire not piloted by Tim.

One new Seafire watched carefully by Haynes, (r)
And if Haynes doesn't keep his nose out of the 'planes,
There'll be no more Seafires watched carefully by Haynes.

There are no more Seafires coming to make a pass, (r)
So Tubby can stick his bats right up his fucking arse,
There'll be no more Seafires coming to make a pass.

CYRIL THE INTREPID BIRDMAN

All hail the intrepid birdman and Cyril was his name,
'Twas in the good ship Khedive that first he made his name,
'Twas a gin tossed night in the wardroom when first he took the air,
The liquor was flowing freely and Navarine   too was there.
He took off by the fireplace, he climbed and soared around,
To the wonder of the multitude all drinking on the ground,
The batsman's name was Shaggers, a drinking man but cool,
But the way he batted Cyril was really "somefink crool",
His height and speed were perfect as he came in to land,
The watching crowd stood breathless for they were all three parts canned.
The batsman raised his arms up and Cyril rose up too,
And then the "Cut" and the silly mutt like an arrow down he flew,
He did not prang the hearthrug but straight to the corticene,
With a muffled bang he made his prang and we saw that he had "Been".

They lifted up the shattered wreck and put it on a chair,
And the very next day in the nice sick bay the doctor did his share.
They put him on the sick list and he's almost better now,
But he's grounded for the duration and I've just told you how,
Beware of drinking batsmen when the wine is flowing free,
And if you let them "Bat" you in you're a better man than me,
So all hail to the intrepid birdman, remember his name with pride,
Who in a gin tossed night in the wardroom, was taken for a ride.

UP AND DOWN THE RUNWAY
(TUNE: So Early In The Morning)

Up and down the runway,
Up and down the runway,
Up and down the runway,
But NEVER in the air.....

**Hummed gently over the R/T during a perimeter track wait,
to the intense nausea of flying control*

GINGER FRAZEELE

CHORUS
G.F., G.F. went to sea in a Swordfish,
Flew over the carrier 66 times,
And was never heard of again,
And was never heard of again

He dropped his syko out at
Southend and it was buried in the sand,
So he could not send a message,
When he was miles away from land.
So listen all you young Observers,
There's a moral to this tale,
Never lose your syko,
Or you will end like Ginger Frazeele.

CHORUS
He forgot to tune his beacon,
As the Stringbag steamed away,
That's why Old Nat Gould and Chandler
Drip about him to this very very day.
So listen all you young Observers,
There's a moral to this tale,
Always tune your beacon,
Or you'll end like Ginger Frazeele.

ARSE-END CHARLIE
(TUNE: "Champagne Charlie")

Arse-end Charlie is me name,
Arse-end flying is me game,
There's no future flying up in front
Unless you're a hero or a silly cunt.

I like flying at the back
I keep weaving when there's flak.
And when there's fighters coming up my chuff
Or if my engine sounds a wee bit duff.

My formation's pretty tight
'Till Japan is out of sight
I don't want to rise to fame,
So Arse-end Charlie I'll remain.

WAVE ME OFF, BOYS
(TUNE: Roll Me Over)

Now this is Number One,
But I've still got too much gun,
Wave me off and send me round
To do it again.

> Wave me off, boys,
> Send me round, boys,
> Wave me off and send me round
> To do it again.

Now this is Number Two,
But I'm way up in the blue,
Wave, etc.

Now this is Number Three,
But lift is down, I see.
Now this si Number Four,
And old Wings is getting sore.
Now this is Number Five.
And I shouldn't be alive.
Now this is Number Six,
And my hook I didn't fix.
Now this is Number Seven,
And I'm half-way up to heaven
Now this is Number Eight,
And I'm floating down the straight.
Now this is Number Nine,
And I think I've had my time.
Now this is Number Ten,
It's the barrier again,
Write me off and dig me out,
I've done it again.

> *Final Chorus:*
> Write me off, boys,
> Dig me out, boys,
> Write me off and dig me out,
> I've done it again.

KATUKARUNDA
(TUNE: Blaze Away)

Insanitary bogs, thieving wogs, got no time for "A" boys,
It's no ruddy wonder that Katukarunda has such a lousy smell,
With lizards and vipers and festering green stripers and negative booze as well,
Go down to dispersal in whites washed in Persil through clouds of dust and sand
Soon you're all gritty and dirty and shitty chuck in your ruddy hand.

If you really want a tossed-out jade
You've got to join the shiny-arsed brigade
If you're fond of whisky and gin and lime
At Katukarunda you've had your time
Shave off Katakurunda's wingless goons.

ONWARD, DEADBEAT PILOTS
(TUNE: Onward, Christian Soldiers)

*A song of the pilots at R.N.A.S. Piarco who flew the pupils
of No.1 Observer School in the skies over Trinidad.*

Onward, deadbeat pilots,
All throughout the war,
Earning much more money
Than you've earned before.
We don't fly for our country,
We don't fly for our King.
But two years in Piarco are
Just the fucking thing!
So .....
Onward deadbeat pilots,
All throughout the war,
Earning much more money,
Than you've earned before.

K.G. V.

We don't care if it rains or snows sir,
We are here to shell Formosa,
Armed with guns from stern to bow,
K.G.V. by Christ, and Howe!

We're not here to fight the Jap sir,
We are here to shoot down C A P; sir
Seafires, Hellcats, muck'em all,
K.G. V is on the ball.

Now it's over, peace at last sir,
Back to Sydney mighty fast sir,
All we've done is sit and talk,
Anson, Howe and Duke of York.

Composed by 820 Squadron after one or two friendly aircraft had been fired on (not always by battlewagons).

To the tune "I am Jesu's little lamb"

THE MARTLET PILOT
(TUNE: Colonel Bogey)

Where was the Martlet pilot when he crashed on deck?
They found one bollock, was in the A.D.P.
The other, was in the deep blue sea.
His whanger was in the hangar,
So tell where can his foreskin be?

THE BARRIER SONG
(TUNE: It's Just Elmer's Tune)

Why does Corbett get morbid and give a dirty look,
When he lands upon the deck and forgets about his hook,
What does Doolan start foolin' and give his bus the gun,
    The Barrier, my son!

Why is Regan just seekin' another place for lust,
Why is Henton just bent on a pilot he can trust,
Why does Mac get the sack from position number one,
    The Barrier, my son!

CHORUS
> *Barrier! Barrier!*
> *It's the biggest bugbear in a Carrier,*
> *Batsmen, crazy,*
> *You feel helpless as you float,*
> *And the Goofers stand and gloat.*

Why is Johnson like a Ronson when he clickers in the gloom,
And he navigates his pilot, almost to his ruddy doom,
Why is Newton away shootin', guess the Monk must have
    his fun,
    The Barrier, my son!

CHORUS:
As for Buster, well he must'a done a lot of time—then some,
And apart from sundry minor faults is really not so dumb,
But if we hang on long enough the time is sure to come,
    The Barrier, my son!

THE MIDDIE'S DILEMMA
(Tune: 'She Had To Go And Lose It At the Astor')

I want to tell you a story, about a young Mid (A) about
17 years of age, about five feet nothing, and about to go up
on his first recce. Now his C.O. realising it was his first time
away from the carrier, called him into the office and said
"Snottie, you're all dressed up in your Irvingsuit, your very
best clothes — if only your Mummy could see you now —
and I want you to remember everything I have ever told you
and above all, I want you to be very VERY careful ... "

But he had to go and lose the old 'Victorious'
He couldn't find the darned ship anywhere
He asked and asked to have a D/F bearing,
But never the faintest sound came o'er the air.

The cabby cursed like hell and quaffed his flagon,
He said the gas was running bloody low,
And if they couldn't find the covered wagon
They'd end up in the hogwash down below.

And all this time the gunner bore up bravely
And carefully examined his Mae West
He thought and thought of how he'd get out safely
When the Albacore upon the waves would rest.

Yes he had to go and lose the old 'Victorious'
He didn't know exactly who to blame
At finding winds he frantically laboured
But each time found the last one not the same.

He tried the spiral searches ten times over
With twists and turns he made the cabby worse
Perhaps it's just as well he wasn't sober
He might have suggested, "Next time bring your nurse".

He'd just about completed all his searches
When in his bunk he sat up with a start
His face was one big beam, for the whole thing was a dream
And he thought that he had lost the old 'Victorious'.

820 SQUADRON'S DANCE
(TUNE: Phil the Fluter's Ball)

Oh have you heard the story of the 820 Squadron's dance,
We didn't do much dancing, but we had some hardy plants,
Everyone was in the Bar, a-propping up the wall,
For all the boys were screeching at 820 Squadron's Ball.

There was bags of beer, music dancing and frivolity
The Squadron's dags had brought their frip and the rest had picked up gash
The people who were dancing were far in the minority,
The C.O. tried to make a speech, and Bobby danced with Bash.

When the ball was nearly over, both the bars were fully packed
Mother Cox shaved off completely when she found her wrens were cacked
In spite of bottles since received, the view shared by all,
Three drunken wrens do not condemn 820 Squadron's ball.

SUNDAY, MONDAY OR ALWAYS

Won't you tell me true —
Can I fly with you
Sunday, Monday or always?

Won't you tell me when
We shall fly again,
Sunday, Monday or always?

No need to tell me that the bloody thing won't go;
No need to tell me that she's flying left or right wing low —

So, if you're satisfied
I will take a ride,
Sunday, Monday or always!

WINTER NIGHTS

Winter nights, that's the time for bombing,
Winter nights, that's the time for bombing,
Let her roar. You're over there once more, and fighting,
Winter nights, that's the time for bombing dear old Mannheim;
Let 'em drop you can't do better
Hear the Huns say "Donnerwetter",
Downstairs, the bombs are falling fast and Huns are running;
Upstairs, you both say "Damn and Blast" with the engines roaring;
And if she 'ends' before you're over Bens, say fellers,
If you understand 'em — you can land 'em,
On those Winter nights.

UNITED STATES MARINES

You can keep your scattered islands
                    and your skies of Asian Blue
You can keep your aircraft carriers
                    and their dim commanders too
You can keep the dusky maidens with
                    their skirts of waving grass
You can keep the whole Pacific
                    and stuff it up your arse.

WIRRAWAYS DON'T WORRY ME

Wirraways don't worry me, Wirraways don't worry me,
Oil chasing bastards with flaps on their wings,
With buggered up pistons and buggered up rings,
The bomb load is so fucking small
Three fifths of five eighths of fuck-all,
There's such a commotion out over the ocean,
So cheer up my lads, fuck 'em all.

They say that the Jap's have a very fine kite,
That we no longer doubt,
When there's a Zero way out on your tail,
This is the way to get out ...
Be cool, be calm, be sedate,
Don't let your British blood boil,
Don't hesitate, shove her right thru' the gate,
And drown the bastard in oil.

A TISKIT – A TASKIT

A tiskit, a taskit, a single engined basket,
They wrote a letter to my Mum
And told her I had crashed it;
I crashed it, I crashed it,
That single engined basket,
I turned on finals, yanked the stick,
Son of a bitch, I snapped it;
I snapped it, I snapped it,
That single engined basket,
A two-turn spin, I torque-stalled in,
Oh Jesus how I smashed it.

EASTERN FLEET SONG
(TUNE: Bless 'Em All)

They say that the Fleet came to Trincomalee,
    Early in 'forty-four,
Heavily laden with men and with gen,
    Bound for the Japanese war.
There's "Vic" and "Indom" and "Illustrious" too,
    The "Indefat" came for the ride.
You get no promotion in the Indian Ocean,
    We'd rather be back in the Clyde.

CHORUS
In the Clyde, in the Clyde,
    Where the runways are half a mile wide,
You get no promotion in the Indian Ocean
We'd rather be back in the Clyde.

They say that the Racecourse is full of fine types,
    And Puttalum's pilots are swell,
The Wrens down at Katukarunda are nice,
    But Minerva's climate is hell.
The Galle Face is galling, the Silver Prawn smells,
    And Kandy's a hellava ride,
You get no promotion in the Indian Ocean,
    We'd rather be back in the Clyde.

The booze is all rationed, the popsies are too,
    The C.O. is getting the twitch,
I've had impetigo, foot-rot, prickly heat,
    And everyone's got Dhobie's itch.
There's Corsairs and Hellcats all over the sky,
    An Avenger's gone over the side,
You get no promotion in the Indian Ocean,
    We'd rather be back in the Clyde.

RUM AND COCA-COLA
(TUNE: Rum and Coca-Cola)

CHORUS:
Drinking rum and coca-cola,
Drink whisky, play tombola,
Brandy's my consola,
Let's fill this ship with alcohola!

The British came to old Hongkong,
And found surrender going wrong,
Instead of signing on "Indom"
The blighters chose the new "Anson"!

Now the "Anson" came from old U.K.,
She broke down three times on the way,
She never fired a shot in anger,
No Kamikaze ever pranged 'er!

Now the "Indom" lay off old Kai Tak,
We must admit she looked a wreck,
The "Anson" gleaming in the sun,
Had never fired a ruddy gun!

When Kamikaze hit "Indom",
Branch types sang this solemn song,
"With enemy we'll come to grips,
Not like these ruddy battleships!"

Day after day, day after day,
It seems that we are here to stay,
And lie rotting 'neath the sun,
With sampans, junks and B.S. one!

Confidentially , it seems to me,
Eventually we'll go to sea,
"Anson" will go to old U.K.,
And I'll bet we go the other way.

ALBERT AND THE WIND

A monologue after Stanley Holloway and 'Albert & The Lion'

'ast 'eard tale of Albert Ramsbotham,
Observer of Makee-learn Squad,
Who knew nowt about navigation,
But just trusted blindly in God?
One day 'e 'ad terrible 'eadache,
'E 'ad too much beer night afore,
'E found 'e was flying that morning
And Albert wi' tongue like the floor.
At briefing 'e took little interest,
In fact it was perfectly plain
That if ever young Albert did get there,
'E'd likely not get home again.
At last Albert's Walrus were airborne
Bare ten minutes late by the clock,
Young Albert 'ad mislaid 'is notebook
And also 'is wind-finding plot.
They'd been flying for nearly three hours,
And suddenly Albert exclaimed,
I think this 'ere kite's going backwards
But I don't see 'ow I can be blamed.
What wind are you using, says Pilot,
It does seem a trifle high?
There's only one wind as I knows of,
That's "Met" wind, was Albert's reply.
The aircraft continued to travel,
And seeing the sea in their track
The pilot was restive wi' Albert,
As 'e didn't know 'ow they'd get back.
At last they saw land underneath them,
And pilot — a lad wi' some skill —
Made excellent landing wi' wheels up,
Red lights showing, 'orn blowing, but still ...
They found they had landed in Ireland.
And for rest of war were interned,
And all 'cos young Albert Ramsbotham
To find 'is own wind 'adn't learned.
Take warning from Albert Ramsbotham,
And never rely on the "Met"
Just find out a wind of your own,
And you'll find that a much safer bet.

WHAT DID YOU DO IN THE WAR DADDY?
(TUNE: Abdul a Bul-Bul)

Oh Daddy what part in the war did you play,
What are the gongs you wear,
Not for firing a gun,
Or sinking the Hun,
But for sinking unlimited beer.

A Pilot my son was your Dad in the war,
A young man who had all the gen,
The wings of the Navy,
With rings that were wavy,
My motto was never say "when".

The worst part was always the waiting my son,
They never could realise the strain,
When poor throats were parched,
How slowly time marched,
Till they started the wine bills again.

A fine upright figure they thought me those days,
With guts and body of steel,
I was reckless and brave,
Ever nonchalant save,
When signing the book for each meal.

But that's not the end of my daring exploits,
Your Father had nothing to hide,
He blitzed Norway's highlands,
Some Japanese islands,
And the Cafe Moderne at Port Said.

The leech ridden jungles were nearly as bad,
As flying and long months at sea,
I was honoured by all,
When I got on the ball,
For none was more whistled than me.

BARRACUDA SONGS

Whatever records the Fairey Barracuda did not
achieve from 1943 onwards, it certainly now holds
what must be a world record for the number of songs
written about any particular aircraft. Despite a
later spell of comparative efficiency in operations
including bombing the Tirpitz, it never got over the
early unpopularity occasioned by the Mark I's tendency
to fold its wings and dive in to the sea, cracked mainspars and
popped rivets on the leading edge, as well as other unfriendly
characteristics. These are well chronicled in song in the
following pages. Many of them are to said to have been
composed on the piano in the ante-room at R.N.A.S. Crail,
which was a Barra O.T.U., and sung while a Board of
Enquiry on the shortcomings of the aircraft was trying
to conduct its business next door in the Wardroom.
Fittingly, perhaps, of nearly 3000 Barracudas built, not
one has survived.

THE NINE WING SONG
(TUNE: These Foolish Things)

That batsman's signals Oh so Vague,
Those long approaches over Ailsa Craig
The sight of many a wreck
A prang on the deck,
Reminds me of FOO.

That Babs that didn't work, that U/S rooster
The sight of Harvey going off the booster
The stolid look of Wings;
These foolish things,
Remind me of FOO.

Biggest boat afloat — you frighten me
Me lifebelt's in my hand whenever we're out of sight of land.

Those evening sessions when we all got plastered,
And drank a toast to Britain's biggest bastards;
Nine Wing is still on the booze.
These shakey does,
Remind me of FOO.

SOMEWHERE A BARRACUDA'S ALWAYS PRANGING
(TUNE: Pedro the Fisherman)

Somewhere a Barracuda's always pranging,
Dive brakes hanging down.
Somewhere a Barra's diving — Merlin banging,
Pilot's pants are brown.
Whistling down towards the sea,
A.L.T., bags of 'G'
Wings will never stand the strain.

Night navigation with the compass on "Setting"
Pilot's getting twitch.
While in the back the "O" and T.A.G. are sweating,
Both are betting 'Ditch'.
Did he have his finger in? Was it gin caused the spin?
Can we blame hydraulics once again?

Frame 25's are cracking, Fairey's slacking,
Large scale sacking due,
But soon we'll have the Barra V
Longer may we stay alive
Then we'll know that Fairey's have a clue.

THEY'RE BREAKING UP BARRA TWOS
(TUNE: They're Digging up Father's Grave)

They're breaking up Barra Twos to build a kettle:
They're doing the job regardless of expense:
They're breaking up Barra's wings,
To build such tiny things
As modern prefabricated tenements.

Would you like to buy a gross of rivets?
We've shed them from St. A.'s to Monifieth;
We haven't had to ditch
But the boys have all got twitch,
And parts are turning brown from underneath, Gaw Blimey!

Won't there be a lot of trepidations?
Alexander's rag-time band will never smile
They pay us six bob a day,
For flogging around the Tay,
Works out fifty quid a bloody mile.

What are they going to do with all the rivets?
They'll pile them all in one great bloody spot;
For the only thing to do
With the Barracuda Two,
Is burn the bloody lot.

OH! MR. AGGIE
(TUNE: Oh! Mr. Gallagher!)

Oh! Mr. Aggie!, Oh! Mr. Aggie!
Is it true the clipped-wing Barra's come to stay?
For this morning in formation, you were slightly out of station
And I saw my starboard wingtip break away.

Oh! Mr. Hoggie! Oh! Mr. Hoggie!
I'm afraid I must agree with all you say,
Wasn't trouble with my vision, but avoiding a collision —
Harry Trimmers Mr. Hoggie! HARRY DIMMERS Mr. A!

Oh! Mr. Aggie! Oh! Mr. Aggie!
Now the next time you are flying in a pair,
You'll recall that Faireys' wings, though they seem quite solid things,
Can't be touched by other wingtips in the air.

Oh! Mr. Hoggie! Oh! Mr. Hoggie!
Now I know that Harry close-ers doesn't pay;
Simply tried to climb a bit, but the wingtips must have hit —
Clipped it nicely Mr. Hoggie! PRETTY DICEY Mr. A!

Oh! Mr. Aggie! Oh! Mr. Aggie!
I've been trained to do dive-bombing for the fleet:
My torpedoes never miss but I'll be as poor as piss
If my Barracuda airframe's incomplete.

Oh! Mr. Hoggie! Oh! Mr. Hoggie!
I was looking in my log book yesterday:
I've pranged tons of bloody shipping, now I've taken up wing-clipping
And I'm sorry Mr. Hoggie! YOU'RE THE BOTTOMS Mr. A!

YOU MUST REMEMBER THIS

*(To the tune of the same name from the Humphrey Bogart
and Lauren Bacall film, "Casablanca.")*

You must remember this — a Barra's poor as piss,
On that you can rely;
No matter what their Lordships say,
It still can't fly.

And when you press the tit, it belches fire and shit,
Right in your fucking eye;
No matter what their Lordships say,
It still can't fly.

Long extended mainplanes, set high above the crate,
High strutted tailplane — very out-of-date,
Woman has man, and the Navy has this Fate
That no-one can deny.

It's still a Fairey story,
A dice with death or glory,
A case of do or die:
The Fleet will always welcome Barras,
When they can fly.

WE DITCH OUR BARRACUDAS
(TUNE: "John Brown's Body")

We've got some fucking aircraft and they ain't no fucking good,
They make 'em out of canvas and they make 'em out of wood,
We fly our compass south when we should be flying north,
And we ditch our Barracudas in the Firth of fucking Forth.

The engine power is negative, the lift is fucking small,
It's a wonder that the fucking thing gets off the deck at all,
We pump our throttle quadrant for all it's fucking worth,
And we ditch our Barracudas in the Moray fucking Firth.

The Barracuda II is a temperamental kite,
It's very fond of spinning in, especially at night,
We learn the fundamentals of our monumental task,
At an outpost of the Empire called Findo-fucking-Gask.

PASSING BY
(TUNE: "Passing By")

There is an aircraft that's brand new,
Called the Barracuda Two,
I did but see one passing by,
But yet I'll fly her till I die.

Vanishing wheels and but one plank,
Fuselage borrowed from a tank,
God only knows how it can fly,
But yet I'll fly one till I die.

D.R. Compass gives you track,
Going out — not coming back,
Pilots who prang them make me cry,
But yet I'll fly them till I die.

FAIREY, FAIREY
(TUNE: Daisy! Daisy!)

Fairey! Fairey!
Give me your answer do:
What is wrong with my Barracuda Two?
Dive-bombing has strained my structure —
I've got a stressed skin rupture,
The rivets pop along the top
And one of them might hit you!

Fairey! Fairey!
What are we going to do?
Nine Wing's grounded — looks pretty bad for you,
When my Barra falls asunder,
I'll be a wingless wonder —
I'll jump out quick and bring the stick —
And stuff it right up your nose!

ANY OLD IRON

Any old iron! Any old iron! Any, any, any old iron!
Talk about a treat torpedoing the Fleet,
Any old cruiser or battleship you meet;
Weighs six tons, no front guns,
Dam' all to rely on,
You know what you can do with your Barracuda Two —
Old Iron! Old Iron!

Any old iron! Any old iron! Any, any, any old iron!
The engine is a teased out Rolls Royce,
A Merlin thirty-two and it ain't our choice,
Open up the throttle and the whole bloody lot'll
Wail like an air raid siren;
You know what you can do with your Barracuda Two —
Old Iron! Old Iron!

Any old iron! Any old iron! Any, any, any old iron!
Tail up high pointing to the sky,
Nobody knows if the blighter will fly;
Your first flight, too much fright,
A kite you can't rely on,
So you know what you can do with your Barracuda Two —
Old Iron! Old Iron!

Any old iron! Any old iron! Any, any, any old iron!
Down at Lee, you can get them free,
Built by Faireys for a crew of three,
Oh what fun, no front gun,
And an engine you can't rely on,
Oh you know what you can do with your Barracuda Two —
Old Iron! Old Iron!

NOTE: Adapted from 809 Squadron's Fulmar Song.

I WONDER WHY?

Some years ago their Lordships thought they'd build a better plane
To go to war;
So Faireys got the order and set out to do again
What they's failed before;
They found all sorts of bits and bobs in old disused workshops,
And bound them all together with the string they pinched from slops,
Then sat and hoped their masterpiece would pass and go on "ops,"
I wonder why?

They'd heard the R.A.F. whose orders never are delayed
Had just passed by,
An engine born of worthy stock which hadn't made the grade
I wonder why;
They stuck it up in front and found they had to raise the tail,
Now if you want a true opinion — take a trip to Crail,
You'll find the boys are hoping that the carrier will not sail,
I wonder why?

For this monster we are flying, Faireys will not take the blame,
I wonder why,
They say they didn't have the time to build a better plane
For us to fly;
This may be true but me and you would ask them for a start
Just where they found the genius who fancied he was smart
And spent a whole year thinking up that two-ton undercart,
I wonder why?

IT'S ALL OVER THE PLACE

It's all over the place.
The Frame twenty five
The wings in a dive
The main spars and flaps.
The stressed skin and gaps —
It's all over the place.

It's all over the place.
It wallows about —
And panels jump out.
A Plane you can't trust.
For the mainplanes soon bust —
It's all over the place.

All round the atmosphere with no control at all
Airframe will shake.
Tailplane will break.
Close the throttle landing on, and like a brick she'll fall —

We ditch
We twitch
We prang the bloody *BITCH.*

It's all over the place
The experts are dim.
They tell us it's trim;
But that's all a lie
For the bastard can't fly
It's all over the place.

I'M DREAMING TONIGHT OF MY BARRA
(TUNE: I'm dreaming tonight of my Blue Eyes)

Oh! I'm dreaming tonight of my Barra,
As I dive her straight into the sea;
Oh! I'm dreaming tonight of my mainplane,
And I wonder if my rivets think of me.

Oh! you told us that we were too cissy,
And by word showed us how to be tough,
And we said we would dive at two-eighty,
But three-fifty you could shove right up your chough!

When the cold, cold waves do enfold me,
Will you stand FOCT and shed just one tear?
Will you say to the gold braid all round you
That the boys you have murdered lie here?

When I'm drawing my harp and my halo,
And my wings that won't fold in a dive,
I will say to the angels around me,
That the rest of the boys will soon arrive.

(sotto voce ... pp)   Oh! I'm dreaming tonight of my Barra,
As I dive her straight into the sea;
Oh! I'm dreaming tonight of my mainplane,
And I wonder if my rivets think of me.

RIVETS FROM HEAVEN
(TUNE: Pennies from Heaven)

Every time it rains
Rivets from Heaven
You'll find rivets falling fast
From Crail to Leven.

And when you dive your Barra
Straight at the ground
Make sure your propeller
Is going round.

Don't wait for your wings to fold,
"Tag", "O" and "I"
Better far to catch a cold —
So — ditch in the sea!

And when those Merlins thunder
Scramble under a tree;
There'll be rivets from Barras
From Crail to Lee.

77

WAY UP THERE IN WHITEHALL
(TUNE: Ragtime Cowboy Joe)

Way up there in Whitehall where Their Lordships are
They travel up to London in an R.N. car.
There they sit and bolster up the worst by far —
The Barracuda Two.
Got their fame by making all our dives so steep —
Still it doesn't make them lose a wink of sleep —
Wherefore should they weep?
Aircrews are so cheap:

So there they sit
While we open the throttle and the tit
Screaming down through smoke and trying to get a hit;
We pop our flaming rivets
But it doesn't really matter just how far the wings we scatter —
THEY'RE ALIVE:
Never seen a Barracuda dive
So how are they going to know
She's a high-wing rootin — rivet shooting
Helluva bitch, that gives you twitch —
The Barracuda Two.

For orders of 2 cases or more further discounts are available on application.

Churchill Graham Lda

OPORTO
PRODUCE OF PORTUGAL.

20% vol.   75 cl.

To place an order either fill in the coupon below or telephone 0171 928 7300/fax 0171 928 4447. Your order will be dispatched to your home or, if you prefer, your business address within 14 days.

McKinley Vintners 7 Burrell Street London SE1 0UN Telephone: 0171 928 7300 Fax: 0171 928 4447

Order Form

Please indicate the quantities you require in the relevant boxes below.

Please make cheques payable to McKinley Vintners.

	Qty	Unit Price	Total
3 bottles	....	....	....
6 bottles	....	....	....
12 bottles	....	....	....
......cases	....	....	....

Delivery Address

Name: ....

Address: ....

....

Daytime telephone number: ....

Preferred payment method: ....

Credit Card Number

McKinley Vintners are pleased to offer the Fleet Air Arm an exclusive limited issue of finest crusted Churchill's port to commemorate the 50th anniversary of VE and VJ days.

A limited issue to commemorate the 50th anniversary of VE and VJ days

CRUSTED PORT

Supplies are definitely not inexhaustable and the following prices are exclusive to attendees:

3 bottles   at   £35.85

WHISTLING DOWN THE RUNWAY
(TUNE: Pistol Packin' Momma)

Whistling down the runway
Finger up his arse.
Someone's got his dive brakes up
Must be dear old d'Arce.

CHORUS:
Put those dive brakes down d'Arce
Put those dive brakes down:
Barra-pranging d'Arcy,
Put those dive brakes down:

Climb to seven thousand
Put her in a dive
First a wail then the tail
Then your bloody guts arrive.

The gunner has twin Vickers guns
The observer he had one
But that ruddy shit in the front cockpit
Has not a bloody one.

Coming in to land her,
Bring old J.C. in.
But that ruddy fart of an undercart
Nearly put you in a spin.

So we'll fly them 'till we die,
And that won't be very long.
For a spot of flak or the wings fold back,
And we'll be where we belong.

WE WANT TO BUY A BARRACUDA
(TUNE: I Want to Buy a Paper Doll)

I want to buy a Barracuda I can call my own,
A kite the R.A.F. will never steal.
And then those whiskered P/O Prunes
With their Mossies and Typhoons
Will have to fly an aircraft that is real.

As through the evening sky we slowly stagger
Just waiting for the next poor sod to die,
I'd rather have a Barracuda I can call my own
Than have an aircraft that can really fly.

SAVE A FIGHTER PILOT'S ARSE

It was midnight in Korea,
All the pilots were in bed,
When up spake General Rogers
And this is what he said:
"Oh pilots, gentle pilots, pilots one and all,
Mustangs, gentle Mustangs, Mustangs one and all".
Then up spake a young Lieutenant
With a voice as bold as brass
And this is what he said:
"You can take those goddam Mustangs Joe
And stick 'em up your arse."

CHORUS:
Halleluja, oh Halleluja throw a nickel on the grass
Save a fighter pilot's arse,
Halleluja, oh Halleluja throw a nickel on the grass
And you'll be saved.

Cruising up the Yalu doing 320 per
Came a call to the Major "Oh, won't you save me Sir
I have two big flak holes in my wings,
My tanks they have no gas;
Oh, mayday! mayday! mayday! got six Migs up my arse."

Fucked up my cross wind landing
My left wing touched the ground,
Came a call from the tower
"Pull up and go around"
I got that Mustang in the air a dozen feet or more
My engine quit — I'm in the shit,
Oh, mayday! mayday! mayday! won't you save me Sir.

I came into the pattern,
To me it looked all right,
My airspeed read 130
My God I pulled it tight,
My engine gave a wheeze,
Mayday! mayday! mayday! — spin instructions please.

801 SONG
(TUNE: Cigarettes and Whisky)

We formed up at Lee in May '52,
Their Lordships said "It's the Far East for you'
Far from the beer sold in old "Keppel's Head".
Work up in Malta, drink Anchor instead".

CHORUS
Engine from Bristols and an airscrew from Rotols,
They drive us crazy, they give us a thirst.
Hawkers supply 'em and we like to fly 'em,
Hoggin' the hours, the Eight hundred and First.

We flew out to Malta, we flew to the Med.,
The troops came the hard way in "Vengeance" instead.
Refuelled at Istres but made a small mess,
We passed 821 who had all gone U/S.

We flew for a couple of months from Hal Far,
Just a few yards from the "First and Last Bar",
The work went well but we got in a rut,
Each Saturday night found the boys down the Gut.

To Barcelona for our summer cruise,
Five nights of women and five days of booze,
Came away feeling more dead than alive,
Ole! the Bull Fight! Ole! District Five!!

Eastward in "Glory" past Aden, and then
When off Malaya they gave us the gen,
Drop bombs in the Jungle throughout the day long,
For this rugged duty we'll give you a gong.

When up the coast we flew all daylight hours,
Flew before dawn and through all the snow showers;
Sorties were much less than two hours long,
But that's far too much when it's near Caeryong.

Cannons went U/S, kept jamming and so
Our armourers worked hard to make the guns go,
C-in-C Far East just hadn't a clue —
The ammo was made in 1942.

Out in Japan we all drank Nippon beer,
Drank it for Christmas and drank it New Year,
But something was added for Christmas wassail —
A pint of McEwans from "The Daily Mail".

The Japanese girls saw they had us in fits,
They flaunted their bodies and showed us their tits;
We were a long way from our home and hearth,
We made up for that with a Japanese bath.

We're leaving Korea at last for a while,
And N.A.2.S.L. is starting to smile,
But from now on until "Glory" passes Nab Light,
Drongo must keep the bar open all night.

821 SQUADRON SONG

At my Lords' annual meeting
With genius so fleeting
They put us together to work as a team;
Led by "Slug" Notley,
We'll fly so shit hotly
We'll be the crack squadron — or so it might seem.

FIRST CHORUS
Sing – hi – ho – thro' space we're soaring
Dreaming of sinking pints back in the pub.
All set for attacking with Ash bombs a clacking
Searching the seas for a sign of a sub.

We formed up at Condor
And there we grew fonder
Of Wren "O's" and booze than we ever had been;
"Slug" said you'll be famous,
If out of my anus
The sun in his glory continues to beam.

FIRST CHORUS

From Iceland to Mackers
We thought we'd go crackers
Six hours to Glasgow by Pony Express;
But by dint of some flying
Hard living, hard lying
We looked on the sheep and we couldn't care less.

FIRST CHORUS

Along came the day
When old "Slug" went away
And after him Nigel, a fucking good bloke;
He said
"You have gone to the dogs
You shouldn't have joined if you can't take a joke".

SECOND CHORUS
Sing — hi — ho — thro' space we're soaring
Months without women are breaking my neck
When you get to Blighty
Remember twice nightly
Bracket the target and fire for effect.

En route to Malta
We had a slight halte
At Istres-le-Tube where the tail wheels went flat;
We went to the village
The women to pillage
But vino and V.D. soon put paid to that.

SECOND CHORUS

At Malta and Gozo
The motto is "Go Slow"
Frustration, repression, is the rule at Hal Far;
So cheer up, me hearties,
And come to our parties.
Bugger the flying, let's buy a new car.

SECOND CHORUS

When the weather was clear
We pranged North Korea
In our Coalburners, — rattling old heaps;
Then, like Little Jack Horner,
We're in Padre's Corner
Telling the lads how we did it "Jeep, Jeep".

SECOND CHORUS

The Commander of "Glory"
Is aged and hoary
"L" san and Pay san are just as old too;
And when drinking's the order
PMO is no hoarder
And East is the beast — completing the crew.

Two Sargents to meet yet are Engines and Air
One's bust his booster, the other's "Grey Hair".

THE BRIEFING SONG
(TUNE: Chatanooga Choo-Choo)

Pardon me chums, there's just a little concentration
Of a hundred Chinese,
Lying under some trees.
So pardon me chums, they need a little quick attention,
Just bombs or R/P's — from a Div. of Furies.

You'll fly to 'X-ray', then to Changyon, up the rail to Sinchon,
Turn north at the Reservoir and make for Sam Bong,
There you'll find the bastards,
Leave them truly plastered,
Feeling pretty buggered and considerably blasted.

Carry out a recce. and report to "Kodak",
Mind the flak positions when you get to Amgak,
How far does the ice go?
Does it reach to Chodo?
'Hello Sitting Duck' — oh, there you are!

Oh, pardon me chums, just keep your sights right on the target,
Just give them a squirt,
And watch those Chinks hit the dirt.
They're going to squeal until they're sure that you will not
                                                    come back,
And for your information we've no new plotted flak.

FRIDAY, THE 13th
(TUNE: Cruising Down the River)

Floating down the Flight Deck
On a Friday afternoon.
That Firefly is far too high,
There'll be a prang here soon.
"Get the jumbo ready";
And old Flyco calls the tune
"Crash on deck — No smoking"
On a Friday afternoon.

The batsman knew
That when he flew
Past him he looked O.K.
But Bacon wished
And then he fished
Then in the barrier lay.

The three of them together
Checked back on the stick too soon,
Bobby, Ted, and Johnny
On that Friday afternoon.

PYONGYANG – A DIRGE
(TUNE: Maryland)

The Chinese is a lucky man o'er Pyongyang, o'er Pyongyang.
The Sea Fury's an "also ran" o'er Pyongyang, o'er Pyongyang.
Both Fireflies and Furies too,
The Migs laugh up their sleeves at you,
And you know well it's bloody true o'er Pyongyang, o'er Pyongyang.

Oh how I hate the Chinese flak o'er Pyongyang, o'er Pyongyang,
It comes up thick and bloody black o'er Pyongyang, o'er Pyongyang.
And if a Sea Fury you drive
And if you wish to stay alive
Don't spare the gas, steer 235 from Pyongyang, from Pyongyang.

In "Ladybird" are sailors too, so very far from Pyongyang,
All dressed up in their Nos. 2 so very far from Pyongyang.
They fuck our women, drink our wine,
For.them this war is bloody fine,
And don't they shoot a wicked line 'bout Pyongyang, 'bout Pyongyang.

And when this bloody war is done o'er Pyongyang, o'er Pyongyang,
There'll be no Mig up in the sun o'er Pyongyang, o'er Pyongyang.
The folks back home will sing our praise,
They'll call us all their heroes brave
And we'll smile back from out our grave at Pyongyang, at Pyongyang.

ON TOP OF OLD PYONGYANG
(TUNE: On Top of Old Smoky)

On top of old Pyongyang
All covered with flak
I lost my poor wing-man
He never came back.

For flying's a pleasure
But crashin' is grief,
And a quick-triggered commie
Is worse than a thief.

A thief will just rob you
And take what you save,
But a quick-triggered commie
Will send you to the grave.

The grave will decay you
And turn you to dust,
Not one Mig in a million
A Fury can trust.

They'll chase you and kill you
And send out more lead
Than cuts in a railroad
Or Migs overhead.

So come all you pilots
And listen to me
Never go to Amgak
Or old Sinwon-ni.

K-9 BLUES
(TUNE: It's Foolish But It's Fun)

Joe wakes us up at break of day,
    He says, "Now fellers, on your way."
No wonder we're all turning grey,
    It's foolish but it's fun.

We race outside, jump in the blitz,
    All wearing our survival kits,
The whole thing gives us all the shits,
    It's foolish but it's fun.

        And if we should have some aborts
          We may get a frown,
        On long escorts, not close supports,
          Usually they're found.

We see a peasant on a farm,
    He looks at us with much alarm,
We'll just leave him our napalm,
    It's foolish but it's fun.

We pull up from a rocket dive
    Indicating ninety-five,
We'll be lucky to survive,
    It's foolish but it's fun.

        And when we call on Mellow,
          To get instructions for a flight,
        If he should say SINUIJU
          We'd die of fucking fright.

He sounds so calm, his voice serene,
    He doesn't know my face is green,
I guess I'm just an old 'has-been',
    It's foolish but it's fun.

Then in to land, I see the deck,
    I wonder if I'll break my neck,
For I black out each time I check,
    It's foolish but it's fun.

Our C.O. works us far too much,
    Three trips a day (or night) and such,
With life we lose our fucking touch,
    It's foolish but it's fun.

In our cockpits there we sit, .
For hours and hours we do our bit,
'Cause if we don't we're in the shit.
It's foolish but it's fun.

Perhaps with a hundred sorties up,
I'll win the D.F.C.,
Perhaps one day I'll get some leave
To Aussie 'cross the sea.

But in the meantime there's no show,
Into the fucking blue I go,
Rain, hail, sleet, or fucking snow,
It's foolish but it's fun.

Now one newcomer's keen to fly,
It's Flight Lieutenant Joey Blyth,
Two hundred hours a month he'd try,
It's foolish but it's fun.

To Iwakuni he recalled,
The poor old bastard nearly bawled,
The thought of flying jets appalled,
It's foolish but it's fun.

He whistled round the circuit
At a hundred bloody knots,
He dreamed of flying Tiger Moths
With slits and slats and slots.

"Those fooking jets may be O.K.,
But I'll take Mustangs any day,
The piston engine's here to stay",
It's foolish but it's fun.

Let Meggsie lead the first attack.
Hunt and Cannon at his back,
And I'll cop all the bloody flak,
It's foolish but it's fun.

With Murphy in his Shooting Star,
And Thornton parted from the bar,
My word these boys will all go far,
It's foolish but it's fun.

One day I'll overstrain myself
And go right overboard,
And com-mit fucking suicide
With a missing razor cord.

Ah, come the day, but until then
　　We'll all press on rewardless, men,
The napalm's mightier than the pen,
　　It's foolish but it's fun.

With Dropkick Easley in the van,
　　These fookin' Chinese up and ran,
And Lyall Klaffer, what a man!
　　It's foolish but it's fun.

Young Les Reading's in the pink,
　　"We'll have another go I think".
Could he mean another drink?
　　It's foolish but it's fun.

　　　　In a corner Scotty Cadan's
　　　　Talking P.R. spits,
　　　　He'd like to photograph Korea
　　　　In little fucking bits.

But for Photo Reccos there's no hope,
　　For the switches we must grope,
Bombs and bullets, that's the dope,
　　It's foolish but it's fun.

Now back upon the bloody deck
　　Why do I risk my fucking neck?
A day to go so what the heck,
　　It's foolish but it's fun.

Our I.O., Ralph, says, "How many trucks,
　　Any tanks, artillery, geese or ducks?"
But I don't give two common fucks,
　　It's foolish but it's fun.

　　　　So bowed and battered, home I go,
　　　　The cause of freedom saved,
　　　　To wake up screaming in the night,
　　　　Dreaming of how I've slaved.

I think to make up for my sins,
　　I'll have myself a dozen gins,
And re-convert to fucking TWINS,
　　It's foolish but it's fun.

UP TO THE PRESENT DAY

THE DRAGONFLY SONG

To 5 Squadron, C. 1957
author possibly AA1 "Lofty" Lipscombe

"Stick-stir in Manual"
Seems to be the favourite cry —
Put it in the seven hundred
Dragonflies aren't fit to fly

And there's also high frequency
Vibration there as well

One-pers, bleed the dampers
Or the kite will fall apart
Clutch will not disengage —
Engine also hard to start.

Boss man says work tonight
Till the job's completed
Soccer players can't be spared
So they'll be defeated.

But — fly the choppers must,
We shall have to shit or bust.

Now we're 'S' for Test Flight,
Send it up into the sky —
Down it comes u/s again,
Hear the pilot's mournful cry

Stick stir in Manual (etc).

RED THREE
by Lt. Scott Lidbetter
(42 Long Twu CSE Song)

(To the tune of the recent hit "Lucille")

Well the briefing was magic
And the take-off was tragic
But into the air we did crawl
9 moved into Battle
The Leader did prattle
He made me feel just 2 feet tall
I did all my sighters
Feeling proud to fly fighters
A film from my hand it did fall
I tried to locate it
I dropped my port wing-tip
As I lost him my leader did call.

CHORUS
You picked a fine time to leave me RED 3
With cloud all around us and broken R/T
Formation renumber
Red 3's made a blunder
I'll screw him you just wait and see
You picked a fine time to leave me RED 3

Well I felt pretty harassed
And very embarassed
But soon got right back on his wing
He called out 'on tow'
I thought 'Here we go'
And started to do my own thing.
I rolled on my back
Looked down through the flak
Of my leader there was not a sign
I said 'Leader where are you?'
He said 'Down here with Red 2
Are you coming down or d'you want us to climb?

CHORUS
Well we finished the sortie
And feeling quite naughty
The leader he said "Follow me'
We bunched and we twisted
And I even wristed
And then I blacked out with the G

Well when I came round
Pointing down at the ground
The leader said 'Red 3 call in'
But there was no way
It wasn't my dav
And Red 3 stoofed in off the spin.

93

"HUGHIE"
(TUNE: Frankie and Johnny)

805 flew from Nowra
To embark for a tropical cruise
We were greeted in Vengeance the right way
The Fish-heads bought plenty of booze
Oh land us on, Hughie land us on.

The Squadron owned Sea Furies
Lordy and how they could fly
'Til they got in the circuit
Then they prayed to the Lord on high
Oh help us on, Hughie help us on.

The batsmen are keen and agile
Performing their witch doctor dance
With leans high-dips and come-ons
The boys don't stand a chance
Oh get us down, Hughie get us down.

Fergie came in for a landing
Flying a little too fast
His hook missed all the wires
He went half up the mast
Oh help him down, Hughie help him down.

We have to get up in the morning
Around about quarter to four
To twitch on the end of a booster
And pour on the old full bore
Oh help us off, Hughie help us off.

Hear the boys bitch in the crew room
Waiting for flying to begin
No need to get excited
The ship's still looking for wind
Oh send some round, Hughie send some round.

The A.D.R.'s really a whizzer
With liner, buster and gate
No need to waste your petrol
The interception's sure to be late
Oh land us on, Hughie land us on.

Fifty one calling Hostage
What's the bogies' angels and course
Wait till we signal to FOCAF
He'll send it back in morse
Oh land us on, Hughie land us on.

Air Sea Rescue's no problem
If in a dinghy you drift
Just wait for McPhee or McMillan
In Bristol's mobile lift
Oh hoist us in, Hughie hoist us in.

Bill is our Senior Pilot
And of him all Subbies beware
They reckon the very first words he spoke
Were "Get into the air"
Oh where's the whip, Hughie where's the whip.

When Al comes over the roundown
To the goofers it looks pretty weird
His seat's so far to the bottom
There's just a flying beard
Oh wave him off, Hughie wave him off.

James made a dart at the flight deck
Nearly went over the side
But there's no foundation in the rumour
That Bevan was hypnotised
Oh keep him on, Hughie keep him on.

Mac's an ace at live bombing
On any target we choose
But to stop the slaughter of wild fowl
He decided not to drop them fused
Tell the Brisbane Press, Hughie tell the press.

Rocketings fraught with danger
When Furies and Fireflies mix
There's no need for flak near a target
When you fly with 816
Oh try again, Hughie try again.

Now we've finished this work-up
We're amazed that we're all still alive
Despite the booster and batsmen
There's still an 805
Oh fly us home, Hughie fly us home.

845 SONG
(TUNE: 'My Bonnie lies over the ocean')

The pingers can't hold their ale lads
We drink just to give them a fright
and when they are on their milkex
well we'll drink on into the night.

CHORUS:
> Oh we'll all pull together
> the 845ths alive
> Oh we'll all pull together
> for flying the Wessex is fun.

Well the junglies are gods gift to flying
a fact that is very well known
we'll fly thro' the worst of conditions
while the pingers are sitting at home.

CHORUS:
> We don't like the task of the Sea King
> A.S.W's particularly dank
> they drop their balls in the oggin
> but we'll use ours for a wank.

CHORUS
> Well we've heard of some other squadrons
> but with us they can't compete
> when it comes to dare-devil flying
> Eight four five are quite the elite.

CHORUS:
> So listen well all you students
> if ever you have a doubt
> of choosing 'tween pinger and junglie
> I assure you that pingers are out.

CHORUS:

Lt. A.S. Cole RN ex 845

FOUR BLADES ON MY WESSEX
(TUNE: 'Four Wheels on my wagon')

Four blades on my Wessex
and I'm still flying along
the Senior P. is after me
but I'm singing a happy song.

Three blades on my Wessex
and I'm still flying along
a throttle freeze I'm in the trees
but I'm singing a happy song.

Two blades on my Wessex
and I'm still flying along
radio's dead, but I'm still ahead
and I'm singing a happy song.

One blade on my Wessex
and I'm still flying along
hydraulics duff, if that's not enough
but I'm singing a happy song.

No blades on my Wessex
and I aint flying no more
fuel and flames, blood and brains
but I'm singing a happy song.

ALPHA TEAM
(TUNE: 'Keep the red flag flying there')

The Bravo team can kiss my arse
I'm in the Alpha team at last
the Senior Pilot shook my hand
the boss told me he thinks I'm grand.
I think I'll take a make and mend
a banyan or a short weekend
the Bravo team can kiss my arse
I'm in the Alpha team at last.

I took the grunts into the air
to take them I just know not where
I flew through a restricted zone
without forewarning on the phone
I over-pitched, I oversped
my needles all went in the red
the Senior Pilot called my name
I'm in the Bravo team again!

PINGER PILOTS LAMENT
TUNE: 'I'm looking over a four leaf clover'

I'm bending over a pinger looker
like I never bent before
I first had a u/c, I then had a wren
but 16 months later it was back to front again

Oh the Senior P.'s complaining
the C.O.'s waning
but I just come back for more
'cos I'm bending over a pinger looker
like I never bent befo..................re.

WESSEX PILOT
TUNE: 'Urban Spaceman'

I'm your Wessex pilot baby, I can fly
I'm a supersonic guy,
I'm your Wessex pilot baby, I've got speed
I've got everything I need.

I don't need systems, or a 5 piece rotor head
And shortly, all the pingers will be going off to bed.

I'm your Wessex pilot baby, I can fly
I'm a supersonic guy.

FAREWELL

Two well-known Aviators are shortening their wings,
They've said goodbye to all of us and turned to other things,
We can't think how this happened, they've hardly reached their prime,
But the wind has blown from the West Land,
As it will from time to time.

CHORUS
Farewell to dear old Gordon,
Farewell to Peter too,
Take care you aged faireys
The next one may be you.

Yes, Peter Twiss is leaving, how sad to see him go,
We'll drink on his expenses at next year's Motor Boat show,
They say that boats are easy and flying isn't funny,
But as you know they loved it so, it wasn't for the money.

We hope they got a handshake,
Silver, gold or brass,
We know just what you're thinking,
And let the next rhyme pass.

THE GOOD SHIP OCEAN

'Twas on the good ship Ocean,
Where Brander had a notion,
Both Fury Squadrons were his aim,
An unpredicted bunch to claim,
But he succeeded just the same,
Aboard the good ship Ocean.

The year of '52 drew on,
All thoughts of going home were gone,
And hence the boss of 898,
Was here-in-after proud to state:
"The squadron will amalgamate" —
Aboard the wicked Ocean.

So East we pushed in search of war,
Glad to sail, Christ knows what for,
We pranged a couple on the way,
And later Pugh was heard to say
"That bloody deck got in the way",
At sea aboard the Ocean.

One night the Captain spun a tale,
All air inside the ship went stale,
"We're off afresh, a mission new,
I send this gen to each of you,
At best it's something new to do,
Aboard the restless Ocean".

So off we went around Inchon,
To land some helicopter on,
The flight and weather decks were cleared,
Goofers all just disappeared,
We're all a shower of shits, it's feared,
Aboard the good ship Ocean.

But soon we're going home for good,
We'd clear off now if e'er we could,
We'll reach Hong Kong and draw our pay,
Before proceeding to U.K.
For Ocean that'll be the day,
Thank Christ it's nearly over.

And hence we came across Japan,
A run ashore with mama-san,
A fairish number thronged the throne,
I wonder, would they, had they known?
The wisest left the thing alone,
A run ashore from Ocean.

When airborne in a later flight,
Young Hick returned to ditch his kite,
Such scares as these you must agree,
Are not the proper things at sea,
But he didn't mind apparently,
Brave deeds aboard the Ocean.

Along came Whitfield in good time,
And more to swell the Squadron's crime,
He flew, it's true, a trip or two,
They say that's what they're there to do,
Of course they love it, wouldn't you?
Aboard the monster Ocean.

Whilst homing on the ship one day,
With "out of focus" C.C.A.,
Pete Sheppard chanced a right hand turn,
A thing that pilots seldom learn,
It caused the "Flyco" great concern,
On board the worthless Ocean.

And when it ended, all went slack,
Our routine from the Med was back,
But L.S.O. suppressed a frown,
Not to mention looks from Brown,
When Hagdorn landed upside down,
Aboard the flat-top Ocean.

Then Gudgeon came upon the scene,
His aim, to get the messdecks clean,
But soon discovered he was getting,
By crawling 'neath the hammock netting,
Dirty knees for not forgetting,
What he found on Ocean.

A.25
Some Rotary verses to the old favourite

They say in the air force a landings okay
if the pilot gets out and can still walk away
but in the Fleet Air Arm the prospects are grim
if the landings piss poor and the pilot can't swim;

CHORUS:
Cracking show, I'm alive
But I've still got to render my A.25

They taught me to fly in a Chipmunk T10
I'd fly round and round and then once round again
the mood of the bird made the landing a farce
so I'd go round again and fly straight up my arse.

CHORUS:
From fixed wing to choppers I quickly moved on
to discover it's safe with no airspeed clocked on
but if your descent is too fast for the flow
then it's chop chop chop chop and away you will go.

CHORUS:
And so front line service I finally saw
the Pilots were good and I viewed them with awe
but found out the maths was just too much for me
and fuck it said Wings some more stores in the sea.

CHORUS:
I led a formation in LFA 2
well lower and lower and lower we flew
forgot the wires on the top of the trees
and a pipe back at camp said let's pray for all three.

CHORUS:

ASHES TO ASHES – THE VIXEN SONG
(TUNE: We're moving on)

1. Hear the pitter – patter of tiny feet,
   It's 892 in full retreat.

CHORUS:
   We're moving on, we'll soon be gone,
   Yeah we get more chops than the choppers and the props,
   We're moving on.

2. Ashes to ashes, dust to dust,
   If the Devil doesn't get you then the Vixen must.

CHORUS:
3. High on the Meatball, throttled right back,
   That was the end of Andy and Mac.

CHORUS:
4. Overshot from an ACR 7,
   Turned downwind on the road to Heaven.

CHORUS:
5. If you don't do your checks, you're a sap,
   Down the cat, panels in your lap.

CHORUS:
6. Nightgloworm – they are out of reach,
   Last recovery on Chesil Beach.

CHORUS:
7. I pull it tight, I've got dash,
   I'm an Admiral's son so I can't crash.

CHORUS:
8. Night cat launches make me frown,
   Selman's O.K. but poor old Brown.

CHORUS:
9. Cress and Jim tried to glo,
   Now they're gone and cold as snow.

CHORUS:
10. Ronald and Rog, made a bog,
    Turned for home and they hit the Og.

CHORUS:
11. Try on the clothes of your late best pal,
    If the cap fits – then wear it Al.

CHORUS:
12.   Chivenor circuit − horsing it round,
      Pulled too hard, and they hit the ground.

CHORUS:
13.   Sometimes you win, sometimes you lose,
      Standby live, it's a V.T. Fuze.

CHORUS:
14.   Now Vixen seats they ain't the best,
      But they sure put the medals on the pilots chest.

CHORUS:
15.   On a 1 V 1, he tried to track,
      But a mountain came between the bogey and Jack.

CHORUS:
16.   Poor little crab − thought the Navy was cissy,
      Went to the Arrows, speared in at Rissy.

CHORUS:
17.   You ain't exempt if you've got three rings,
      You don't fly a Prince if its only got wings.

CHORUS:
18.   First cat launch on a Friday morn,
      Over − rotated and Bruce was gone.

CHORUS:
19.   There was Alec and Pip in the goldfish bowl,
      Looked out the window, − God rest their souls.

CHORUS
20.   Captain and Padre at the door,
      "Oh", says the wife "What a goddamn bore".

CHORUS:
21.   Dust to dust − ashes to ashes,
      We all get pissed, and another one crashes.

CHORUS.

THE VIXEN SONG

Picture if you can, a Vixen
   Rushing through the starry skies,
Picture, too, the intrepid pilot
   Peering through his bloodshot eyes.

Long ago he joined the service,
   Said he'd like to learn to fly —
Thought it meant some easy money,
   Rich retirement bye and bye.

Thought as well of babes and popsies,
   And the glamour of those wings.
Or visits to exotic places,
   Parties, dances, other things ...

Now he sits in frozen terror,
   Bathed in moonlight's cheerless glow;
Trying not to think of landing
   On that flight deck down below.

Tiny deck, enormous airplane
   Guided by his hands and feet.
In the darkness none to tell him
   How on earth the twain shall meet.

His alone the great decisions,
   He the Captain of his fate.
Life itself the constant wager
   'Gainst the snares that lie in wait.

But stay, there *is* one guiding hand
   To lead him in the paths of right.
One voice to lend encouragement
   When fear strikes deep at dead of night.

For on his right, and just behind him,
   Shielded from plebeian view,
Dwells within the Vixen's bowels
   A second member of the crew.

Trained in the arts of navigation,
   Versed in interception lore;
Master-mind and shrewd tactician
   When the Vixen goes to war.

This is he they call the Looker,
   Silent partner of the team,
Thinker extraordinary
   Of the cream the very cream.

Aided by his electronics,
   Helped by radar's probing eye;
His vital task the skilled direction
   Of the Vixen around the sky.

Master, too, of relaxation
   Soothing words and healing balms,
Oft-times in the air he wanders
   'Wrapt in Morpheus' Blissful arms.

Then it is the wrathful pilot
   Bellows forth in angry roar,
Only to be answered with
   A small observatorial snore.

At last the moment comes for landing,
   When the Looker's work is done.
When his special tasks are ended
   And his test of faith begun.

Now in turn the pilot needs
   Must wake from dreams and concentrate,
While the ATCO talks him gently
   Down towards the homing gate.

Through the gate and join the pattern,
   Cockpit checks and lights all green.
Throttle back and down the glidepath
   Till the meatball's clearly seen.

Closer still and o'er the round-down:
   Now the time for faith and prayer.
Hold the airspeed, check the line-up:
   Nearly down ... A bright red flare!

Keep your head now, throttles open!
   Take your bolter like a man.
Climb away and keep her level,
   Visual circuit if you can.

Down-wind leg and check the fuel,
   One more pass and that's your lot.
On the meatball, keep her steady,
   Steady, steady, steady, ZOT!

Down at last, a perfect landing,
   Model of the pilot's art.
Now see the carefree crew emerge
   With sweating brow and pounding heart.

See them weaving down the flight-deck
   Twitching gently, faces green,
Reporting to the Senior Pilot:—
   "Normal sortie — just routine."

THREE WHEELS ON MY VIXEN

Three wheels on my Vixen,
And I'm still flying along.
Flyco there is after me,
Sure is mad, that's too bad,
'Cos I'm singing my happy song.

CHORUS:
Oh Lordy.

Two wheels on my Vixen,
But I'm still flying along.
Left my tyre in the wires,
Barrier's gone their last one,
But I'm singing my happy song.

One wheel on my Vixen,
But I'm still flying along.
Right hand seat, not a peep,
Pulled his cord and up he soared,
But I'm singing my happy song.

No wheels on my Vixen,
And I ain't flying no more.
Hit the deck, what a wreck,
Fire and foam, flesh and bone,
But I'm singing my happy song.

A VIXEN'S MADE FOR PITCH UP
(TUNE: These Boots are made for Walking)

You keep saying that you're pretty steely,
That there's nothing flying that you can't hack,
But one day you'll overstep the line child,
And that's when a Vixen's gonna bite right back.

CHORUS:
'Cos a Vixen's made for pitch up,
And that's just what it'll do,
And one of these days a Vixen's
Gonna pitch right up on you.

Pull it really hard and tight on finals,
Hear the Looker babbling with fright,
Speed 120 add's a burbling,
But still you manfully call out "on sight".

Well you tell how much you love flying,
But the way you're flying now fills me with gloom,
And when in the wreckage they find you a-dyin'
They're gonna write these words upon your tomb:

FAIREY AVIATION COMPANY
(TUNE: The A.25 Song)

We've flown for a living, but also for fun,
And never relaxed till the work was all done,
But now that we're leaving we earnestly say,
It's a marvellous life and to hell with the pay.

CHORUS
Cracking show, it's all past,
For the Gannet Mk. 3, they all say is the last.

When sinking the Bismarck, the Swordfish was there,
From our Civil hangar it took to the air,
A very fine action, a very fine swirl,
But that man Kenneth More got away with the girl.

Confronted at first with a Barra Mk. One,
When designers and stressmen have finally done,
We turned to the Foreman and said "Tell me Jack,
Which is the front end and which is the back?

The Firefly flew with remarkable grace,
An engine, a tail, and between them some space,
From a piloting viewpoint the finest design,
Was that Ringway production, the unmanned Mk. 9.

The Gannet was splendid, it went to the Fleet,
It worked very well and they thought it a treat,
The choppers came in and the Gannets went out,
Then the Choppers went in with a fine waterspout.

When Faireys invented triangular shapes,
We pilots got into some perilous scrapes,
But Four figured flight came, and here are our thanks
For it put us ahead of those four-lettered Yanks.

The Gannet Mk. 3 is the last they are sure,
We think it's been pregnant for eight months or more,
That radome's suspicious I'll bet two pounds ten,
That we've started production all over again.

We have to end up without tears in our eyes,
And let you all in on a lovely surprise,
We saved all our pennies and now we have got,
Enough to buy Westlands, the whole bloody lot.

NOTE
Written at the time of the Westland takeover in 1960.

THE DIRGE OF 849
(TUNE: Eton Boating Song)

They're lowering the standards for Aircrew,
General List Officers as well,
Observers get lost in the BUNDU,
And Pilots get drunk in the BELL

CHORUS
Oh! We'll all pull together,
The A.48 as well,
Oh! we'll all pull together,
For flying the Gannet is hell

They're lowering the standards for Aircrew,
Pilots who can't read or write,
By day they just sleep or drink coffee,
And go GAFFING women at night.

They're lowering the standards for Aircrew,
Men you won't normally meet,
They get drunk on Brandy and Whisky,
And they park COOKIES right in the street.

They're lowering the standards for Aircrew,
Don't know how an aeroplane works,
It's all this new co-education,
At school they just learn to lift skirts.

They're lowering the standards for Aircrew,
Some pilots act quite strange and coy,
This often confuses the M.O.
Who can't decide if SHE'S a BOY.

They're lowering the standards for Aircrew,
It's all dirty books, film shows too,
They ask fifteen shillings to see them,
We all pay our cash — wouldn't you?

They're lowering the standards for Aircrew,
Lowsee and mutuals by night,
By day we do Distrike and Recce,
All work and no play — is it right?

They're lowering the standards for Aircrew,
It's all sex and drinking and mirth,
Ask the Boss what he'd do as a C.O.,
He'll say — 'Have them strangled at birth'.

Now all you young maidens forgive us,
If we seduce you — or worse,
Don't blame the poor men, blame the system,
For standards go on getting worse.

THE BUCCANEER SONG
TUNE: *The Gasman Cometh*

'Twas on a Monday morning, the first launch was at eight
Six Vixens were to be launched, but five of them were late,
There was panic up in flyco, they did not know what to do,
So they launched the five spare Buccaneers to do what Vixens do.

CHORUS: *Oh it all makes work for the Buccaneers to do-oo-oo-oo-oooo*

'Twas on a Tuesday morning, a Gannet on low-see,
Sent to find a Krupny, which was far out at sea,
When suddenly his APS—20 went for a ball of chalk,
So they called upon the Buccaneers to do the Gannet's work.

'Twas on a Wednesday morning, the Choppers should have dunked,
But they got their balls in a twist and the sorties would have flunked,
When someone shouted "801 — they've never known defeat"
So they called upon a Buccaneer with its underwater seat.

'Twas on a Thursday morning, there was some mail ashore,
The courier was in FLY ONE, U/S, would fly no more,
The engineers were working hard 'twas all to no avail,
So they called upon the Buccaneers to go and fetch the mail.

'Twas on a Friday morning the tankers could not fly,
The Army wanted air support but nobody knew why,
We launched an "on call" Buccaneer — that ever useful plane,
And flew ashore and blew the wogs to hell and back again.

Now Saturday and Sunday are our days of rest,
The Vixens and the Gannets on the flight deck doing tests,
The Buccaneers are down below all handsome and sedate,
Awaiting Monday morning when the first launch is at eight

SIX NIGHT TRAPS
TUNE – *Sixteen Tons*

CHORUS
You do six night traps and what do you get,
Fully night qualified, and covered in sweat,
Now Wingsy don't you bug me, 'cos Little 'F's enough,
If you want to fly in 'ARK ROYAL', you've gotta be tough,

1. I was born one night on the end of Zero – Nine,
    The Taxi -- lights weren't working, the Meatball didn't shine,
    My Daddy was Venom Pilot, so I heard tell,
    My Mummy was a Wren who the Aircrew called Nell.

CHORUS
2. One night we threw the L.S.O. over the side,
    A lot of men had heeded him, a lot of men had died,
    Wreckage on the Flight Deck, metal, oil and foam,
    And back on the Round – Down, there was flesh, blood and bone.

CHORUS
3. Sometimes a man gets weary with the Staff all around,
    Always critising with their feet on the ground,
    SAVO and FOCAS – makes a boy cry,
    Just ancient bums who've forgotten how to fly.

CHORUS

MEATBALL WIZARD
(*TUNE: Pinball Wizard*)

1. When I was a young sprog, the Goofers I'd enthrall,
    'Hermes', 'Vic' and 'Centaur', I guess I've played them all,
    But never did one good D.L. – at least that I recall,
    That deaf dumb and blind kid, – Sure flies a low Meatball.

2. Horsing round on finals, see that Meatball sink,
    Better stuff some power on, or wind up in the drink,
    Amid the cries of the Goofers, hear the lonesome Looker call,
    That deaf dumb and blind kid, – Sure flies a low Meatball.

3. I've seen them low, I've seen them high,
    I've seen them hit the ramp,
    I've seen them screw on overshoot, and get their backsides damp,
    I've seen the fear leap to their eyes when they hear that
    'Bolter' Call,
    Those deaf dumb and blind kids, – Sure fly a low Meatball.

THE LONESOME MEATBALL.
(TUNE – "The Reverend Mr Black")

1. He rode tall in his Bang Seat, a Man among Men,
   He'd even go to briefings every now and then,
   When he rolled out on Finals, he was always slow,
   And folks just called him the Squadron Joe.
   He never read his Pilots Notes, he didn't know a thing,
   And sometimes below the Glidepath you could hear him sing.

CHORUS.
   You've gotta fly that lonesome Meatball,
   You've gotta fly it by yourself,
   There ain't nobody going to help you,
   You've gotta fly it by yourself.

2. If ever I thought that the Squadron Joe,
   Was a yellow kind of so – and – so,
   I threw away that notion on a cold dark night,
   When he hit the Ramp and took away the Sight,
   He hit the deck like the kick of a Mule,
   And to my way of thinking it took a damn fool,
   To keep on flying in that busted wreck,
   And turn downwind for a pass at the Deck,
   But up in Flyco amid the gloom,
   You could hear a voice echo round the room,
   And it said,

CHORUS
3. Its been many years since we had to part,
   I guess I learned his ways by heart,
   "Don't argue with me boy – I'm always right,
   Fly the Deck – ignore the Sight".
   Do I remember him? indeed I do,
   'Cos I was the Squadron Joe's Number Two,
   And sometimes around Sundown you'll hear him cry,
   From that great big Flight Deck up in the Sky,
   And he says,

CHORUS

THE BALLAD OF WINGSY BABY
(Dedicated to Cdr D. Monsell R.N.)
(TUNE: "Big Bad John")

1. Every morning at Flyco you could see him arrive,
   He stood 5'10", weighted 195,
   Shouted and cursed, blustered and swore,
   Till everyone said "I can't take no more".
   From Wingsy Baby.

CHORUS:

Wingsy Baby, Wingsby Baby,
He drives me crazy.

2. No-one really knew where Wingsy came from,
   Some said he'd been a Lumberjack in Saskatchewan,
   He just kind of stood there, looking big and mean,
   The perfect computorised decision machine,
   Was Wingsy Baby.

CHORUS:
3. "Monsell's Laugh-in"' they called the first launch,
   With Wingsy presiding there was bound to be a graunch,
   "Why's he bolted" he'd shriek, waving at the skies,
   "We've only just launched him", Flyco replies,
   To Wingsy Baby.

CHORUS
4. He walked into Briefing with the air of a 'Wheel',
   And wait for the ATCO to finish his spiel,
   Then with a crashing blow from a big right hand,
   Sent the whole goddam briefing to the Promised Land,
   Would Wingsy Baby.

CHORUS:
5. "When you're Chicken, divert," the Good Book says,
   But thems ain't the rules our Wingsy plays,
   But we forgave him his foolish ways,
   Since he based his figures on Sea Hawk days,
   Did Wingsy Baby.

CHORUS:
6. I caught three wire, feeling cool and calm,
   Heard Wingsys' voice like a soothing balm,
   "Thats a tight enough circuit, boy,
   Keep it that way",
   But I'd just landed off a CCA.

CHORUS:
7. "Now you just fly that Meatball, and stay Centreline,
   And catch those wires at 139,"
   Yes the people gathered round from near and far,
   To hear Wingsy brief the SAR.

CHORUS:

8.   "Now who'd like a trip with Wingsy today?"
'92's Duty Boy was once heard to say,
There was screaming, shouting, riots and more,
And God help the Looker who drew the short straw,
With Wingsy Baby.

CHORUS:

9.   And then one day the Yankees came,
To talk about tactics and the name of the game,
There was shouting and cursing from way out front,
And a Yank was heard to say "Who the Hells that ————?"
(Thats Wingsy Baby).

CHORUS:

10.   Now 809 and 892 had a few late nights last week,
Thats true,
But that there ain't no Squadron Joe,
That snoring coming from out the front row,
That's Wingsy Baby.

CHORUS:

11.   But then in August, he left his Throne,
Panic turned to fear and Goofers turned to stone,
So tremble and shake all you aircrew on board,
'Cos we traded in Wingsy for a 'Second Hand Ford'.

CHORUS.

THE L.S.O. SONG
(TUNE: "I've been down so long it looks like up to me"
—Nancy Sinatra)

1.   He walks the deck, his board beneath his arm,
He says "My son, you'll do yourself some harm,"
"That Wave-off nearly put you in the sea,"
I've done Reds so long they look like Blues to me.
(Repeat last line).

2.   Well ten yards out he called me "Lined up right",
But still I put my Port Wing through the Sight,
"You adjust on line-up a shade too positively",
I've done Reds so long they look like Blues to me.

3.   He stands before me trousers tattered and torn,
And talks about my third wave-off that morn,
But his canvas escape 'chute was at the laundry,
I've done Reds so long they look like Blues to me.

4.   He tries to help with every modern aid,
But he's lost count of the foul-ups that I've made,
His wave-off lights are switched on constantly,
I've done Reds so long they look like Blues to me.

113

THE FOUR FOUR WIRES OF HOME
(TUNE: 'The green green grass of home')

1. The old deck looks the same.
    As I come down through the rain,
    And there to greet me in Flyco, all a 'screamin',
    Pass the ramp I go, lined up right now,
    L.S.O. shrieks "Fly the sight now",
    As again I miss the four four wires of home.

CHORUS:
    Yes they'll all come to see me,
    All laughing, smiling sweetly,
    As again I miss the four four wires of home;

2. The Bolter's still the same,
    But the Looker he ain't there now,
    And I turn downwind with fuel state down on Chicken.
    high in close, I take a cut now,
    "Wave off, wave off", youve made a F---- now,
    As again I miss the four four wires of home.

CHORUS:
3. *(To be recited with the mass ensemble of 892 & 809
    cooing gently in the background).*

    Then I awake and look around me,
    At Six Xray that surrounds me,
    And I realise that I was only dreaming,
    For there's a Duty Boy and Senior Pilot wittering,
    And come the dawn they'll drag me twittering,
    Across that deck, across those wires of home.

A SHIP WITH NO BOOZE
TUNE: *"A Pub with no beer"*

1. Well it's lonesome away from your kindred and all,
   On the Flight Deck at night, where the lone Goofers call.
   Could death be better? It's so hard to choose,
   When you serve in a ship where they don't let you booze.

2. Yonder stands the C.O., He's God's rep on Earth,
   He'll give the bar bollocks, show his lads what he's worth,
   Two Pink Gins later he's dragged screaming away,
   "Will-yarm", says the Commander, "Thats enough for today".

3. Now Gerry the SOBS, he can just sit and glower,
   Tries to make his H.N. last for an hour,
   He'd hoover them down, but he's on a go slow,
   Two paces behind him stands the P.M.O.

4. The A.W.I. walks in with a dry dusty throat,
   Walks up to the bar for a twin rum and coke,
   When the barman won't serve him he turns the air blue,
   "Sir we only serve Fisheads — we don't serve Aircrew.

5. Chris Bolton's a Crabfat— On his first cruise,
   And after two weeks they removed his booze,
   He went to the C.O., his heart felt like lead,
   "It's a limit, not a target", was what the Boss said.

6. Here stands young 'Tooty', '92s bon viveur,
   Man about bars and entrepreneur,
   His soul is sickened, he wants 'out' from this boat,
   'Cos the Admiral won't let him throw ale down his throat.

7. Farewell to O'Connor — he's leaving the 'Ark',
   Considerably dryer than when he embarked,
   There's one consolation in this teetotaling hell,
   Its excellent practice if you're going G.L.

8. The 'Quiffy' crawls in, his goon suit all torn,
   He's just had a Ramp Strike, his nerves are all worn,
   "Pray give me a brandy" — a pathetic cry,
   But the staff are so wet — thats why the 'Ark' is so dry.

9. Extensive studies throughout the Air Arm,
   Prove that boozing and flying need not cause alarm,
   When flying your Phantom low over the sea,
   The ideal blood count should be two-forty-three.

10. Well it's lonesome away from your kindred and all,
    On the Flight Deck at night, where the lone Goofers call.
    Could death be better? It's so hard to choose,
    When you serve in a ship where they don't let you booze.

115

HEY HO SAYS ANTHONY WIGLEY

A: Is for Aircrew, the men who can think. Hey ho says Wigley
B: For the Bar where we all sit and drink
        With a roly poly
        Up em and stuff em
        Hey ho says Anthony Wigley
C: Is for C—King, Built to go ping. Hey ho etc etc.
D: Is the D who just cant do a thing. Chorus.
E: Is for Engineers, Who like their pits. Hey ho etc.
F: Is for flyco, who gives us the shits. Chorus.
G: Is for Gannet that tries to sink subs. Hey ho etc.
H: Is for Hangar, where Aeo grubs. Chorus.
I: Is for injection from Ark Royals quack. Hey ho etc.
J: Is for Jolly-hog, raines leads the pack. Chorus.
K: Is the LBO, hurling abuse. Chorus
M: Is for MLA always in doubt. Hey ho etc
N: Is the NAV who is always way out. Chorus
O: Is for OPS, who is all piss and steam. Hey ho etc
P: Is the programme thats always a dream. Chorus
Q: Is the Quarts of H.N. that we drink. Hey ho etc.
R: Is the Radio, again on the blink. Chorus.
S: Is for S.O.B.S. who doesn't like chat. Hey ho etc.
T: Is for training, we're all sick of that. Chorus
U: Is the URGE that we try to contain. Hey ho etc
V: Is the VIRGIN we dream of in vain. Chorus
W's The wind that is outside the graphs. Hey ho etc
X,Y,Z You can stuff up your arse. Chorus

I'M A SEAKING CHAP (Lumber jack song)

GROUP A: I'm a Seaking chap and I'm O.K.
           I fly all night
           And I sleep all day.

GROUP B: He's a Seaking chap and he's O.K.
           He flies all night
           And he sleeps all day.

GROUP A: I go to brief
           I get dressed up
           With mae west and a boat
           And if I ditch my SEAKING
           I hope like hell I float.

GROUP B: He goes to brief
           He gets dressed up
           With mae west and a boat
           And if he ditched his SEAKING
           He'd hope like hell he'd float.

BOTH GRPS: He's a SEAKING chap and he's O.K.
He flies all night
And he sleeps all day.

A: I stay aloft
I fly around
For four long hours or more
And when its time to charlie
My arse is BLEEDIN' SORE.

B: He stays aloft
He flies around
He four long hours or more
And when its time to charlie
His arse is BLEEDIN' SORE.

BOTH: He's a SEAKING chap etc etc

A: I get undressed
I bath and scrub
And then go to the mess
I drink my nine tots daily
And seldom have much less

B: He gets undressed
He bathes and scrubs
And then goes to the mess
He drinks his nine tots daily
And seldom has much less

BOTH: He's a SEAKING chap etc etc

A: I eat my food
I drink my ale
I've put on several pounds
But if the doctor weighted me
He'd keep me on the ground.

B: He eats his food
He drinks his ale
He's put on several pounds
But if the doctor weighted him
He'd keep him on the ground.

BOTH: He's a SEAKING chap etc etc.

A: I hate grey ships
I hate fixed wing
I hate the whole damned scene
I'm only really happy
When I fly my machine.

B: He hates grey ships etc etc
BOTH: He's a SEAKING CHAP etc etc.

ASSORTED ODES

Oh the wigley wogley men
They dont get up till ten,
They give a shout,
And run about,
And go back to bed again.
Oh the wigley wogley boys
Have put away their toys,
Give them a beer,
And you will hear,
They make a lot of noise,

AMONG MY SOUVENIRS

1. Theres nothing left for me.
    But cups of hot, strong tea.
    Beers just a memory,
    Among my souvniers

2. An old wine bill or two,
    An R.P.C. from you.
    Hangovers, not a few,
    Among my souvenirs

3. A coke does not seem right,
    To help me fly at night.
    And coffee after flight,
    Brings me no consolation.

4. My body breaks apart,
    And then the tear drops start,
    I find my GOOD PUBS chart,
    Among my souvenirs.

SOBS DREAMS OF SHAKESPEARE

Once more into the dip, 54, once more
Or forever roam out sector counting green grenades;
For nothing more becomes a crew than TIGHTLIP
            (Cept the stories)
But when a racket is within a hundred miles
Then out with the plotting boards, gage, transition up,
And dangle our thingies forty miles ahead,
Crying GOD FOR SOBS, ARK, and 824.

LESBE FRIENDS
(TUNE: The farmer and the cowboy should be friends).

CHORUS: Oh The aircrew and the fisheads should be friends,
Oh The aircrew and the fisheads should be friends,
The aircrew and the fisheads
The run rats and the piss-heads,
But there aint no reason why they cant be friends.

1 I'd like to say a word for the seamen
They suck their teeth and dip their bread in gravy
How does your cable grow
Dirty Bastards, we all know
For Nelson said that Arsehole rules the navy.

CHORUS

2 I'd like to say a word for the stokers
Dont criticise them for their lousy manners
For stokers are no fools
They've a lovely set of tools
And they sweat upon their nuts with King-Dick spanners.

CHORUS

3 I'd like to say a word for the Greenies
They spend their lives in air-conditioned spaces
They think its very camp
When they talk of OHM and AMP
And put on all their mincing airs and graces

CHORUS

4. I'd like to say a word for the stovies
They've spent their last six years in trepidation
In spouting lots of wazz
And talking through their ass
They really are the queens of aviation!!!!

CHORUS

5. I'll leave the final word for 824
Our skin is soft, our hair is long and wavy
But when it comes down to the crunch
We're a well endow'ed bunch
We've got the biggest goddammed choppers in the navy 1

FINALE: Oh. flight deck folks should be friends
Flight deck folks should all be chums
Flight deck folks should stick together
Never ever talk to the fishead bums!!!!

824 SECOND—PILOTS SONG

1.   I am an unrated co-pilot,
     I always sit here on the left.
     My mind is quite firmly in neutral,
     My thumb firmly stuck up my ....
(Chorus)............... FRC's make good reading,
     Read them by day and by night,
     For if you dont know them by heart son,
     You'll always end up in the ....
     .... Sweet violets,
     Sweeter than the roses,
     Covered all over from head to toe,
     Covered all over in sweet violets.

2.   The first pilots mind is a mystery,
     His flying is really a farce,
     I wish I could take his green rating,
     And shove the thing right up his ....
     .... FRC's etc.

4.   The crewman should be far more wary,
     For his life is full of pit-falls,
     To wake him I cry LOWER THE BODY,
     But he sits there and dangles his ....
     .... FRC's etc.

THE CHANNEL ONE BLUES
(Or, What do I have to do to get a landing spot?)
TUNE: Grand Cooley Dam

1.   Xray Sierra flyco this is Seaking Oh - five - two

     I've sat here in the starboard wait at least an hour or two
I'm getting low on fuel, Oh flyco wont you speak
I'd rather land upon fly three than sit here all dam week.

2.   Five-Two this is flyco we're in an awful mess

The Buccaneers are bolting and a Phantom's in the nets
A Gannet's stuck half up the lift its getting out of hand
You'll have to stick around some more there ain't no room to land.

3.   X-Ray Sierra flyco this is Seaking Oh-Five-Two
I've got a massive oil leak, hydraulic failure too
The engines have stopped turning and the water's getting near
Flyco won't you tell me, when will the deck be clear?

4.   Five-Two this is flyco, now don't break out in tears
There isn't any evidence to justify your fears
Just keep that chopper flying, don't let it come to grief
You're not allowed to ditch the thing, it isn't in your brief.

5.   X-Ray Sierra flyco your last was just too late
We're sitting in the water now, still in the starboard wait
It's true a chopper flier's life is not a happy one
But we will still be flying when the last fixed wing has gone.

*Ark callsign: GRXS

GIVE ME THE ARK NECESSITIES
(TUNE: The bare necessities of life)

CHORUS: Give me the Ark necessities
                The simple Ark necessities,
                Forget about the worry and the strife.
                Give me the Ark necessities,
                Like Phantoms, Gannets and Buccaneers,
                And then you've got the story of my life.

1.   Wherever I wander, wherever I roam,
I got no deck space to call my own,
They always land me on fly—3.

The soot comes wafting down on me,
When I look down,
I'm a healthy brown,
Its the quickest tan this side of town,
The Ark necessities of life aren't what I need.

2.   I love those movies, that I can't see,
Two hundred heads are in front of me,
I stand up and bump my head,
So I got to bed instead,
But I have to sleep,
Piled up three deep.
She's the Q.E.2 of the western fleet,
These Ark necessities of life aren't what I need.

3.   I fly Ark Airways to earn my pay,
When I'm not sleeping 8 hours a day,
Just to put the picture right,
I must also sleep at night,
So you'll have to wait,
If your mail is late,
'Cos the bar and I have a regular date,
The Ark necessities of life may come to you.

GENERAL ODES
AND DITTIES

ARSEHOLES ARE CHEAP TODAY

Arseholes are cheap today, cheaper than yesterday,
Small boys are half a crown standing up or lying down;
Larger ones are three and six, 'cos they take larger dicks,
And one at five bob for a very large knob.

Some are wreathed in smiles others are sore with piles,
The one for me, is the one that's free.
Tallyho, Tallyho, what a lovely sight,
Half a mo, half a mo, whilst I have a shite.

ABDUL A BUL-BUL AMEER

The harems of Egypt are fair to behold,
The maidens the fairest of fair,
The fairest was Greek, she was owned by a Sheik,
Known as Abdul A Bul-Bul Ameer.

A travelling brothel that came to the town,
Owned by a Russian who came from afar,
He offered a challenge to all who could shag,
As Ivan Skavinsky Skavar.

Now Abdul rode by with his snatch at his side,
His eyes flamed with a burning desire,
And he wagered ten thousand that he could out-shag
This Ivan Skavinsky Skavar.

They came on the track with their tools hanging slack,
The starter's gun punctured the air,
They were quick to the rise, and all gaped at the size
Of Abdul A Bul-Bul Ameer.

Although Abdul was quick at flicking his dick,
And the action was learnt by the Czar,
He couldn't compete with the long steady beat,
Of Count Ivan Skavinsky Skavar.

Now Ivan had won and was polishing his gun,
And bent over to polish his pair,
When he felt something pass up his great hairy arse,
It was Abdul A Bul-Bul Ameer.

The harlots turned green, then men shouted "Queen",
They were ordered apart by the Czar,
But Abdul, fuck his luck, had got himself stuck,
In the arse of Skavinsky Skavar.

Now the cream of the joke, when apart they were broke,
Was laughed at for years by the Czar,
For Abdul, the fool, had left half his tool,
In the arse of Skavinsky Skavar.

ANTHONY ROLEY

A is for Arsehole all covered with shit,
   "Heigh ho!" says Roley
B is the Bastard who longs to get there,
   Singing "Roley Poley, Gammon and Spinach,
   Heigh Ho!" says Anthony Roley.
C is for Cunt all slimy with piss, singing ...
D is the Drunkard who gave it a kiss, singing ...
E is for Eunuch with only one ball, singing ...
F is for Fucker with no balls at all, singing ...
G is for Gonorrhoea, goitre and piss, singing ...
H is the Harlot who fucks when she's sore, singing ...
I is the Injection for clap, pox and syph, singing ...
J is the Jump of the bastard up bitch, singing ...
K is the King who shat on the floor, singing ...
L is the Lecherous licentious whore, singing ...
M is the Maiden all tattered and torn, singing ...
N is the Noble who gave her his horn, singing ...
O is the Orifice, tall, deep and wide, singing ...
P is for Penis all peeled down one side, singing ...
Q is the Quaker who shat in his hat, singing ...
R is the Roger who rogered the cat, singing ...
S is the Shithouse that's filled to the brim, singing ...
T is the Turd that is floating therein, singing ...
U is the Usher at a virgin girl's school, singing ...
V is the Virgin who played with his tool, singing ...
W is the Whore who thought fucking a farce, singing ...
And X, Y and Z you can stick up your arse, singing ...

THE BALL OF KIRRIEMUIR
(Just a few verses)

CHORUS: *Singing Fal dae it this time, fal dae it noo,*
          The one that did it last time, canna do it noo.

  OR: *Balls to your father, arse against the wall,*
          If you've never been fucked on a Saturday night,
          You've never been fucked at all.

It was the ball, it was the ball, the ball of Kirriemuir
Four and twenty pairs o' breeks were scattered on the floor.

Up got aged veteran who fought among the Boers,
He jumped upon the table and cried aloud for whores.

There was fuckin' in the haystacks, there was fuckin' in the ricks,
Ye couldna' hear the pipin' for the swishing o' the pricks.

125

Four and twenty old maids, came o'er from Aviemore.
Only one of them got hame and she was double-bore.

Four and twenty virgins were sitting in a row
Pulling at their pubic hairs and passing round the po.

The Elders o' the kirk were there and they were shocked to see,
Four and twenty maidenheads hanging from a tree.

The Session Clerk oh he was there, it was a crying shame,
He'd rode a lassie a' the nicht then wouldna' take her hame.

The Church Precentor he was there, he came in trews o' tartan,
They didna' like the colour but he said "twas done by fartin".

The farmer's son, oh he was there and he was in the byre,
Inducing masturbation with an india rubber tyre.

Miss McHaggart she was there, she kept them all in fits,
By jumping off the mantlepiece and landing on her tits.

The village Bobby he was there, he'd on his fancy socks,
He fucked a lassie forty times then found she had the pox.

The minister's wife, oh she was there, she was the best of a'
She stuck her arse agin the door and bad them come awa'

The minister's skivvy she was there, she was all dressed in blue
They tied her to a barn door and bulled her like a coo.

The postie's daughter she was there, all draped up in the front,
Wi' poison ivy up her arse an' a thistle up her cunt.

The doctor's wife, oh she was there; she wasna' very weel,
For she had to mak her water in the middle o' a reel.

The butcher's wife, oh she was there, she also wasna' weel,
For she had to go and piddle after every little feel.

Jock McGregor he was there, in a new Ford truck,
They asked if he'd hae a dram but he said he'd rather fuck.

Roon aboot the washing house and in among the ricks,
Ye couldna' see a blade o' grass for balls and standing pricks.

Mr. McFudge the parson, he went among the women,
He took puir Nellie on his knee and filled her full of semen.

John Broon the facter, he didna' think it shame
To dance a bloody hornpipe upon a lassie's wame.

Jock, the sweep, oh he was there; they had to throw him oot,
For every time he farted, he filled the room wi' soot.

The village looney he was there, he was an awful ass,
He went into the granary, and stuffed his arse wi' grass.

Farmer Tamson he was there, he sat doon and grat,
For forty acres o' his oats were fairly fuckit flat.

There was fuckin' in the barnyard and fuckin' in the laft,
But one auld wife of eighty-five was nic't against the shaft.

The plumber and his mate were there, they had it in their rules,
When comin' to attend the ba' not to forget their tools.

Jean McPherson, she was there; she cowped wi' a dunt
And all the folk rejoiced to see her muckle hairy cunt.

Four and twenty virgins came doon frae Inverness,
And when the ba' was over there were four and twenty less.

First lady forward, second lady back,
First lady's finger up the second lady's crack.

The village idiot he was there a-makin' like a fool
By pulling his foreskin over his head and whistlin' through his tool.

Old farmer Jock and he was there to see what they were at
He had a forty acre field a-fairly fucked flat.

Little Willie, he was there, he was only eight,
He could not fuck the women, so he had to masturbate.

The Teacher frae the school was there, she didna' bring her stick,
She wasna' much to look at, but could she take the prick.

The village blacksmith he was there, he was a mighty man,
He had two balls between his legs that rattled as he ran.

The village postie, he was there — he had a dose of pox,
He couldna' get a woman so he fucked the letter box.

The village cripple, he was there; he wasna' up tae much,
He stood the girls agin the door and fucked 'em wi' his crutch.

The bride was in the bedroom, explaining to the groom
The vagina, not the rectum, was the way into her womb.

The King was in his counting house, counting up his wealth;
The Queen was in the parlour a-playing with herself:

Jock McBride, he was there, a-sittin' on a stool
Three of the legs were wooden, and the fourth one was his tool.

The village vicar he was there, to fucking wouldna' stoop,
They say he's keen on buggery, since he joined the Oxford Group.

The Vicar's daughter she was there, a lousy little runt,
With roses round her arsehole and barbed wire round her cunt.

The village pro was there as well, up to her usual tricks,
Swinging from the chandeliers and landing on men's pricks.

Now Mrs. Steward, she was there, she was the worst of all,
In the bed, oot the bed, up against the wall.

The grocer's wife she was there, she had a novel stunt;
Poison ivy round her neck a carrot up her cunt.

The Intelligence Officer he was there frigging in the hay,
Feeling in his pockets for the letter of the day.

The M.T. Officer he was there, his girl was by his side,
Filling in a 658 before they had a ride.

There was fucking in the parlour, fucking on the stairs
You couldna' see the carpets for the cunt and curly hairs.

And when the ba' was over, the ladies all expressed
They'd all enjoyed the dancing but the fucking was the best.

And noo the ba' is over, and a' are on their ways
Excepting Meg McPherson who's coming through her stays.

THE BASTARD KING OF ENGLAND

The minstrels sing of an ancient King,
Who lived long years ago,
He ruled his land with an iron hand,
And his ways were mean and low.
He was very fond of hunting, within the Royal Wood,
He was very fond of apple pie and pulling the Royal Pud,
He was fat and forty and full of fleas,
And the Royal Tool hung down to his knees,
        Cheers for the Bastard King of England.

Now the Queen of Spain was an amorous dame,
An amorous dame was she,
She loved to fool with the Royal Tool,
Of the King across the sea.
So she sent a Royal message by a Royal messenger,
To ask the King to come and spend a month in bed with her.
        Fun for the Bastard King of England.

Now Philip of France he shat his pants
When this news to him was brought,
He said "She loves my rival,
Just because my tool is short."
So he sent the Count of Zipitizap,
To give the Queen a dose of clap.
        Meant for the Bastard King of England.

When the news of this foul deed was brought,
To England's ancient Halls,
The King he swore by the Royal whore,
To have King Philip's balls.
So he offered half his kingdom and a fuck at Queen Citance,
To the Loyal, Royal son-of-a-bitch who would bugger the
King of France.
        Good for the Bastard King of England.

So the Noble Duke of Sussex,
He galloped across to France,
He swore he was a Nancy, so
The King took down his pants.
Then he fastened a thong round the Royal prong,
Mounted his horse and galloped along,
        Back to the Bastard King of England.

Now all the whores of London were lined up on the walls,
When told to shout for the Bastard King the harlots shouted "Balls".
And the King threw up his breakfast, and grovelled on the floor,
For in the ride the Frenchman's pride
Had stretched a yard or more.
So Philip of France usurped the Throne,
His sceptre was the Royal bone.
        The end of the Bastard King of England.

BRIAN BORU

CHORUS: *Hi g'lee, hi g'light,*
It's a bloody fine song I could sing it all night.

Now talking of fucking well fucking's all right,
I once fucked a girl forty times in a night,
And each time I fucked her I shot her a quart,
If you don't call that fucking you fucking well ought.

Now old Mrs. Riley she had a dun cow,
To milk that brown beastie she didn't know how.
She pulled on its tail instead of its tit,
And poor mother Riley got covered in shit.

Young Mary McGuire was a whore of renown.
The tracks of her arse were all over the town.
Her tariff was fourpence she never charged higher,
Fair fuck was the watchword of Mary McGuire.

Now Barny O'Flynn was a lad you should meet,
He'd clap from his head to the soles of his feet.
A globule of mercury hung from his chin,
"Begob oi am rotten" said Barny O'Flynn.

Young Brian Boru was a foine sort of lad,
There wasn't a stricture that he hadn't had.
And when he made water 'twas orange and blue,
" 'Tis the ould oirish colours" said Brian Boru.

A policeman was walking one day on his beat,
When he heard a commotion way down on the street.
He turned round the corner and looked up on high,
And a can of hot shit hit him right in the eye.

He looked to the East and he looked to the West,
And another great turd hit him right on the chest.
He looked to the North and he looked to the South,
And a fucking great lump hit him right in the mouth.

That policeman was angry, that policeman was sore,
He called Mrs. Riley a clap stricken whore.
And now at the end of our street does he sit,
With a card round his neck saying "Blinded by shit!"

THE CHANDLER'S BOY
(TUNE: Lincolnshire Poacher)

The Boy went into the Chandler's shop
Some matches for to buy
He looked around, around he looked,
But no one did he spy.
He cried aloud, aloud he cried
With a voice to wake the dead
When he heard a kind of a "Rat-tat-tat"
                    right above his head
When he heard a kind of a "Rat-tat-tat"
                    right above his head

Now the boy was of an inquiring mind
So he quickly climbed the stair
And the door of the room was open
And the Chandler's wife was there.
The Chandler's wife lay on the bed
A man between her thighs
And they were having a "Rat-tat-tat"
                    right before his eyes,
And they were having a "Rat-tat-tat"
                    right before his eyes.

Oh Boy, Oh Boy, my secret keep
And for me tell a lie,
For if the Chandler should hear of this
He'd beat me till I cry.
And if you promise to be good
I'll always to you be kind
And you shall have a "Rat-tat-tat"
                    whenever you feel inclined
And you shall have a "Rat-tat-tat"
                    whenever you feel inclined.

The Chandler returned and entered the shop,
He quickly smelt a rat,
Seeing his wife all naked there
Her hand upon her twat.
The Chandler's wife ran to the room
Expecting the Boy had fled,
But he was having a "Rat-tat-tat"
                    all by himself in bed
But he was having a "Rat-tat-tat"
                    all by himself in bed.

CATS ON THE ROOF TOPS.
(TUNE: John Peel)

CHORUS: *Cats on the roof tops, Cats on the tiles,*
Cats with syphilis, Cats with piles,
Cats with their arseholes wreathed in smiles
As they revel in the joys of copulation.

The Donkey is a solitary moke
He very very seldom gets a poke
But when he does, he lets it soak
As he revels ... etc.

Hippopotamus so it seems
Very seldom has wet dreams
But when he does he comes in streams
As he revels ... etc

Poor old Bovine, poor old Bull
Very seldom gets a pull
But when he does the cow is full,
As they revel ... etc.

Poor little tortoise in his shell
Doesn't manage very well
But when he does he fucks like hell
As he revels ... etc.

Now the hairy old Gorilla is a sedentary ape
Who very seldom does much rape
But when he does he comes like tape
As he revels ... etc.

Bow-legged women shit like goats
Bald headed men all fuck like stoats
While the congregation sits and gloats
And revels ... etc.

Now I met a girl and she was a dear,
But she gave me a dose of Gonorrhea,
Fools rush in where Angels fear
To revel ... etc.

When you wake up in the morning and you're feeling full of joy
And your wife isn't willing and your daughter isn't coy
Then you've got to use the arsehole of your eldest boy
As you revel ... etc.

When you wake up in the morning with a ten inch stand
And there isn't any woman in the whole of the land,
Then there's nothing for it but to use your hand
As you revel in the joys of copulation.

THE BOY STOOD ON THE BURNING DECK

The boy stood on the burning deck, his arse against the mast,
His arse against the mast,
He said he would not move a step till Oscar Wilde had passed,
Till Oscar Wilde had passed.

*CHORUS: Star of the evening pretty little evening staaar,
Star of the evening shining on the shithouse door.*

But Oscar was a wily bird he threw the boy a plum,
He threw the boy a plum,
And when he went to pick it up he leaped upon his bum,
He leaped upon his bum.

But the boy was up to all the tricks, he'd been to Public School,
He'd been to Public School,
He gave his pretty arse a twist and fractured Oscar's tool,
And fractured Oscar's tool.

CHIN CHIN – CHINAMAN

Chin Chin Chinaman, walking down the Strand,
Stony-broke, wants a poke, penis in his hand,
Up comes Posy Lil, he doesn't care a rap,
Three days later, CLAP, CLAP, CLAP!

COCAINE BILL

Cocaine Bill and Morphine Sue
Walking down 5th Avenue

CHORUS: *Honey have a (sniff) have a (sniff) on me*
           Honey have a (sniff) on me

Said Cocaine Bill to his Morphine Moll
There ain't no sense in alcohol

From Broadway to the state of Maine
They went in search of more Cocaine.

They came to a drug store painted green
The sign outside said 'No Morphine.'

They came to a drug store painted red
The sign it said Try Coke instead.

They went down to the riverside
And there committed suicide.

Now in the graveyard on the hill
Lies the body of Cocaine Bill.

From ashes to ashes and dust to dust
If the Lord don't get you the cocaine must.

Now this little story goes to show
There is no sense in sniffing snow

Praise my soul it is the Lord
Coming in to land at Ford,
Listening out on Channel 'B'
Singing honey have (sniff) have a (sniff) on me.

COME ON BOYS

Come on boys drinks all round, let's have a jolly good supper.
One man in bed with another man's wife is a fool if he doesn't
Send his boys to school, send his boys to school,
Before he's learnt his ABC he's playing with his tool.
Mrs. Murphy had two rabbits one of them a buck,
She put them in a rabbit hutch to see if they would
Rule Britannia two monkeys up a stick,
One put his finger where he should have put his
P stands for pudding, R I stands for rice
C U stands for something else it's naughty but it's
Blackpool is the place for me, there's fishing and there's rock,
I never use my fishing rod, I always use my
Pretty little finger so slender and so slim,
I can get all five of them inside my girlfriend's
Pockets are so useful when you're out of luck,
Do not spend your last three ha'pence on a damned good
Turkish bath and manicure to make yourself look smart,
When you're at the dinner table never let a
Swear word pass your lips please refrain from humming
Do not tell your best girl so even when you're
Coming to the Station yard to see the engines shunt,
A piece of steel flew off the wheel and hit her in the
Country Girls are pretty lying in the grass,
They kick their legs up over and show their dirty
Ask old Brown to supper, ask old Brown to tea,
If he doesn't come just tickle his bum with a stick of celery.
Cock a doodle doo, cock a doodle doo,
If he doesn't come just tickle his bum with a cock a doodle doo.

DAHN THE PLUG 'OLE

A woman was bathing her baby one night,
The youngest of seven — the poor little mite;
The muvver was poor and the baby was fin,
'Twas only a skeleton covered wiv skin.

The muvver turned round for the soap on the rack,
She was only a moment, but when she looked back
'Er baby 'ad gorn. In anguish she cried;
"Oh, where is my baby?" The angels replied:
"Your baby 'as gorn dahn the plug;
Your poor little fing was so tiny and fin,
It should 'ave been barfed in a jug.
Your baby is perfectly happy,
You won't see its face anymore,
Your baby 'as gorn dahn the plug'ole,
Not lorst — Just gorn before.

135

CRAVEN A

Listen to my story kindly if you will
About a bastard born in Muswell Hill
Born in Muswell Hill but spawned in Camberwell
And the first words he spoke were "Bloody Fucking Hell".

CHORUS
Craven A never heard of copulation
Craven A never dipped his tool
Craven A quite content with masturbation
Thought a cunt was something you were called at school

OR

Craven A never heard of copulation
Craven A never had his greens
Craven A quite content with masturbation
Fooling with his foreskin in the school latrines.

Now Jenny was a prostitute of Cambridge town
She gamarouched a Proctor in his cap and gown
And then she told that Proctor which she didn't ought
That she'd never seen a bastard with a tool so short.

Now the Proctor very quickly up and told that whore
He'd a cousin who had never seen a cunt before
And he wrote to Craven A saying quickly pack your things
For the shooting season opens on the fourth at Kings

Craven's entry to the Varsity was quite grotesque
He went and laid his penis on his tutor's desk
His tutor said, "Please bring it at a later date
I'll be very glad to use it as a paper weight".

The Proctor said to Craven "One thing I must impress
Never masturbate in academic dress
But Craven just to show he didn't give a fuck
Tossed himself off in the teapot shouting "that's for luck".

Now quickly Craven found that after they had dined
All the undergrads line up for what they call a grind
So he hid beneath the bed despite the awful smell
And when the others came Craven came as well.

Now Jenny had a daughter who was small and wee
She used to take her cunt up with the morning tea
Now he's through her so often that the courts declare
Her vagina constitutes a legal thoroughfare.

Up in Belfry sexton stands,
Pulling pud with grimy 'ands.
Down in vestry Vicar yells
"Stop pulling pud – pull fooking bells!"

'Andsome butler, pretty cook
Down in pantry 'aving fook.
Up in parlour mistress squeals
"Stop fooking cook – cook fooking meals!"

Out in garage chauffeur lies
Firmly clasped by Mistress' thighs.
Master says "Ah there you are,
Stop fooking wife – start fooking car!"

THE FOGGY DEW

When I was a bachelor I lived all alone,
And I worked at the weaver's trade,
And the only only thing that I ever did wrong,
Was to woo a fair young maid.
I wooed her in the summer time,
And in the winter too,
And the every every time that I took her in my arms
Just to save her from the foggy foggy dew.

One night she came to my bedside,
When I lay fast asleep,
She put her head upon my breast
And there she began to weep.
She wept, she cried, she damn near died,
She said, "What can I do?"
So I took her into bed and covered up her head,
Just to save her from the foggy foggy dew.

Now I am a bachelor and I live with my son,
And we work at the weaver's trade,
And the every every time that I look into his eyes,
He reminds me of that fair young maid,
He reminds me of that summer time,
And of the winter too,
And of the many many times that I took her in my arms,
Just to save her from the foggy foggy dew.

ESKIMO NELL

When men grow old and their balls grow cold, and the tips of their knobs turn blue,
They dream of a life midst Yukon strife, and they tell you a tale or two.
Now give me a seat and give me a pint, and a tale to you I'll tell
Of Dead Eyed Dick, and Mexican Pete and a harlot named Eskimo Nell.

Now, Dead Eyed Dick and Mexican Pete had been working Dead Man's Creek,
And they'd had no luck in the way of a fuck for well nigh over a week.
A moose or two, a caribou, a bison cow or so,
But Dead Eyed Dick, with his mighty prick, had found the fucking slow.

So Dead Eyed Dick and Mexican Pete set out in search of fun,
And it was Dead Eyed that packed the prick, and Mexican Pete the gun.
They blazed a trail, that randy pair, their course no man withstood,
And many a bride who was hubby's pride, knew pregnant widowhood.

They hit the Strand of the Rio Grande at the height of a blazing noon,
And to quench their thirst and to do their worst, they sought Black Mike's saloon.
They crashed the swing doors open wide and both prick and gun flashed free,
Accordin' to sex, you bleedin' wrecks, you drinks or fucks with me!"

Well, they knew the ways of Dead Eyed Dick from the Grande to Panama
So with nothing worse than a muttered curse those dagos sought the bar.
The women too knew his playful ways, down on the Rio Grande,
So forty whores pulled down their drawers at Dead Eyed Dick's command.

They saw the fingers of Mexican Pete clench on his pistol grip
So they didn't wait, but at a hurried rate, those whores began to strip.
And Dead Eyed Dick was breathing quick with lecherous snorts and grunts
For 40 arses were bared to view, to say nothing of 40 cunts.

Now 40 arses and 40 cunts, you'll see if you use your wits,
And if you're quick at arithmetic, makes exactly 80 tits,
And 80 tits is a gladsome sight to a man with a mighty stand,
It may be rare in Berkeley Square but not on the Rio Grande.

Now Dead Eyed Dick was in fighting trim as he backed and took a run
And made a jump at the nearest strump and scored a hole in one
He bore her to the sandy floor, and fairly fucked her fine,
Although she grinned, it put the wind up the other thirty-nine.

Well, Dead Eyed Dick he finished quick and he flung the first aside,
And he made a dart at the second tart when the swing doors opened wide
And into that hall of sin there came, into that harlot's hell,
A lusty maid who was ne'er afraid, and her name was Eskimo Nell.

Dead Eyed had got his prick well into number Two
When Eskimo Nell let out a yell and gave a loud "Hey you!"
He gave a flick of his mighty prick and the girl flew over his head,
With a snarling shout he turned about, both his face and his prick were red.

But Eskimo Nell, she stood it well, she looked him between the eyes,
With a look of scorn for the mighty horn that rose from between his thighs.
She puffed a jet from her cigarette over his steaming knob,
And so taken aback was Mexican Pete he forgot to do his job.

It was Eskimo Nell who broke the spell, in accents clear and cool,
"Why, you cunt-struck simp of a Yankee pimp, d'you call that thing a tool?"
And this here town can't take it down" — she glanced at those cowering whores,
— "Well, there's one little cunt that can do the stunt, and it's Eskimo Nell's — not yours!"

She stripped her garments one by one with an air of conscious pride
Till forth she stood in her womanhood and they saw the Great Divide
It's fair to relate, 'twas not too great, but full of feminine vim:
And a better word, which is sometimes heard, would not be cunt, but quim.

Now Dead Eyed Dick had seen this trick so he just took his time,
A wench like this was fucking bliss, so he played a pantomime.
He flicked his foreskin up and down and made his balls inflate,
Until they resembled the granite knobs that stand at a garden gate.

He winked his arsehole in and out and his balls grew twice their size,
His mammoth prick grew twice as thick and reached up to his eyes.
He polished it up with alcohol just to make it steaming hot,
And to finish the job he sprinkled the knob from a Cayenne pepper pot.

Nell flexed her knees with a supple ease and she spread her legs apart,
And with a friendly nod to that randy sod she gave him his cue to start.
He didn't push at her hairy bush, or take a flying leap,
He didn't swoop, but got down to a stoop and a steady forward creep.

As a gunman might he took a sight along that steaming tool,
And the dead slow way he put it in was calculating cool.
Nell took it in right up to her chin and gripped him like a vice,
But Dead Eyed Dick he rattled her like a set of liar dice.

But Eskimo Nell was an infidel and she equalled a whole hareem,
She'd the strength of ten in her abdomen and a rock of ages beam.
Amidships she could stand a sea like the flush of a water-closet,
So she gripped his cock like the Chatswood lock of the National Safe Deposit.

Well, you've seen the mighty pistons on a giant C.P.R.
With a driving force of a thousand horse, then you know what pistons are,
Or you think you do, but I'm telling you, you've yet to learn the trick
Of the work that's done on a non-stop run by a man like Dead Eyed Dick.

Dead Eyed Dick would not come quick, he meant to reserve his powers,
For when he had a mind he could grind and grind for a couple of solid hours.
But Nell lay awhile with a blissful smile, then the grip of her cunt grew keener,
And then with a sigh she sucked him dry with the ease of a vacuum cleaner.

She performed this feat in a way so neat as to set up a grave defiance
To the primary cause of those basic laws that govern sexual science.
She grimly rode through that Phallic Code that for years had stood the test,
And the ancient rules of ancient schools in a moment or two went west.

And now, my friends, we near the end of this copulatory epic;
The effect on Dick was neat and quick, 'twas akin to an anaesthetic.
As he fell to the floor, he knew no more, his passion extinct and dead,
His tool flopped out with one last spout which surely stripped the thread.

Now Mexican Pete jumped to his feet to avenge his friend's affront,
And his long nosed Colt, with a jarring jolt, he shoved right up her cunt.
He leaned his hip on the pistol grip and fired, twice times three,
But to his surprise she closed her eyes and smiled in ecstasy.

"Why, bully" she said, as she raised her head, "Why, bully" she said "for you,
Though I might have have guessed that that was the best that pimps like you could do
When next, my friends, you two intend to go out in search of fun
Buy Dead Eyed Dick a sugar-stick, and buy yourself a bun.

For I must go back to the frozen North, where the pricks are hard and strong,
Back to the land of the mighty stand where the nights are six months long.
It's hard as tin when you get it in, in the land where spunk is spunk,
Not a dribbling stream of lukewarm cream, but a solid frozen chunk.

Back to the land where they understand what it means to copulate,
Where even the dead sleep two in a bed and the infants masturbate.
Back again to the land of men where their spunk comes as thick as gum,
Where my knees shall bend for a worthy end, for the North is calling "Come".

LULU

Some girls work in factories, some girls work in stores,
But Lulu works in a knocking shop with forty other whores.

CHORUS:
Bang it into Lulu, bang it good and strong,
Oh what shall we do for a good blow through when Lulu's dead and gone?

Lulu had a baby, she called it Sonny Jim,
And put him in the pisspot to see if he could swim.

First he went to the bottom, then he came to the top,
Lulu screamed and lost her head and grabbed him by the cock.

I wish I were a wedding ring upon my Lulu's hand,
And every time she wiped her arse I'd see the promised land.

I wish I were a pisspot under Lulu's bed,
For every time she pissed in it I'd see her maidenhead.

The rich girl uses vaseline, the poor girl uses lard,
Lulu uses axle grease and gets it twice as hard.

Lulu joined the WRNS they sent her to the front,
It wasn't the lead that killed them dead but the smell of Lulu's cunt.

LILIAN

Her name was Lilian, she was a beauty
She lived in a house of ill repute;
Fellows came from miles around to see
Lilian in her deshabille.

She was lovely, she was fair,
She had lots of golden hair,
She drank lots of demon rum,
Smoked hashish and o-pi-um.

Day by day Lilian grew thinner
Insufficient vita-min-her
She grew great hollows in her chest
Had to go round completely dressed.

Lilian's troubles started when
She covered up her abdomen
Clothes may help a man go far
But they're just no use to a *fille-de-joie*.

Lilian went to her phy-sician
He prescribed for her condition
He said you've got, I regret to say,
Per-nish-i-ous an-ae-mi-a.

She ate lots of vitamins
She ate starch and pro-te-ins
She ate starch and she ate yeast
But still her clientele decreased.

Her old admirers lasted awhile
But soon they tired of a hollow smile
Lilian died soon of starvation
Through complete lack of remuneration.

That was the story of a girl named Lilian
She was one girl in a million
This is the moral of Lilian's sins
Whatever your profession
                    FITNESS WINS.

AN ODE TO THE FOUR LETTER WORDS

Banish the use of the four letter words
Whose meanings are never obscure.
The Angles and Saxons, those bawdy old birds,
Were vulgar, obscene and impure.
But cherish the use of the wheedling phrase
That never says quite what you mean;
Far better be known for your hypocrite ways
Than as vulgar, impure, or obscene.

When Nature is calling, plain speaking is out,
When Ladies, God bless 'em, are milling about.
You may "Wee-wee", "Make water", or "Empty the glass",
You can "Powder your nose", even "Widdle" may pass.
"Shake the dew off the lily", "Phone your Grandma",
"See a man about a dog" — you've not gone too far.
But please to remember, if you would know bliss,
That only in Shakespeare do characters "......"

A woman has "Bosoms", a "Bust", or a "Breast",
Those "lily white swellings" that bulge 'neath her vest
Are "twin towers of ivory" — "sheaves of new wheat",
In moments of passion "ripe apples to eat".
You may speak of her nipples as "fingers of fire"
With hardly a question of raising her ire,
But I'll bet you a bob she'll throw two thousand fits
If you speak of them blandly as good honest "......"

It's a "cavern of joy" you are thinking of now,
A "warm tender field awaiting the plough".
It's a "quivering pigeon" caressing your hand,
Or the "National Anthem" (it makes us all stand!)
Or perhaps it's a "flower", a "grotto" or "well",
"The hope of the world", or a "Velvety Hell",
But friend, heed the warning, beware the affront
Of aping the Saxon — don't call it a "......"

Though the lady repels your advances, she'll be kind
As long as you intimate what's in your mind.
You may tell her you're "hungry", you "need to be swung",
You may ask her to see "how your etchings are hung",
Or mention the "ashes that need to be hauled",
"Put the lid on her saucepan", even that's not too bald,
But the moment you're forthright, get ready to duck
For the wench isn't weaned who'll stand for "Let's ......"

So banish the words that Elizabeth used
When she was the Queen on the throne.
The modern maid's virtue is easily bruised
By the four letter words all alone.
Let your morals be loose as an Alderman's vest
If your language is always obscure;
To-day, not the act, but the word is the test
Of the vulgar, obscene or impure.

FRANKIE AND JOHNNY

Frankie and Johnny were lovers,
Lordee how they could love,
Swore they'd be true to each other,
True as the stars above,
He was her man — but he done her wrong.

Frankie and Johnnie went walkin',
Johnny in a brand new suit,
Frankie went walkin' with Johnny,
Said "Don't ma Johnny look cute?
He is my man, wouldn't do me no wrong."

Frankie went down to the corner,
Went for a bucket of beer,
Frankie said to the bartender,
"Has Johnny, my lover, been here?
He is my man, wouldn't do me no wrong!"

"Don't want to cause you no trouble,
Don't want to tell you no lie,
I saw Johnny 'bout an hour ago
With a girl called Nelly Bligh,
He is your man — but he done you wrong!"

Frankie went down to the hotel,
She didn't go there for fun,
'Cause underneath her kimono
She toted a 'forty-four gun.
He was her man — but he done her wrong.

Frankie pulled back her kimono,
Pulled out the old 'forty four,
Root-a-toot-toot, three times she shot,
Right through that hardwood door,
He was her man — but he done her wrong.

"Roll me over gently,
Roll me over slow,
Roll me over on my left side,
'Cause your bullets they hurt me so,
I was your man — but I done you wrong."

"Bring out your rubber tyred hearses,
Bring out your rubber-tyred hack,
I'm taking my lover to the graveyard,
And I ain't going to bring him back,
He was my man but he done me wrong."

Sheriff called next morning"
Said it was all for the best,
He told her that Johnny her lover
Was nothing but a doggone pest.
He was her man but he done her wrong.

Frankie said to the Warden,
"What are they going to do?"
The Warden he says to Frankie,
It's the 'lectric chair for you.
He was your man — but he done you wrong.

This story ain't got no moral,
This story ain't got no end,
This story just goes to show,
That there ain't no good in man:
He was her man — but he done her wrong.

FARTING CONTEST

I'll tell you a tale that is sure to please
Of a grand farting contest at Shitton-on-Tees
Where all the best arseholes paraded the fields
To compete in the contest for various shields.

Some tightened their arses to fart up the scale
To compete for a cup and a barrel of ale,
While others whose arses were biggest and strongest
Took part in the section for loudest and longest.

Now this year's event had drawn a big crowd
And the betting was even on Mrs. McLeod,
For it has appeared in the evening edition
That this lady's arse was in perfect condition.

Now old Mrs. Jones had a perfect backside
Half a forest of hairs with a wart on each side,
And she fancied her chance of winning with ease
Having trained on a diet of cabbage and peas.

The vicar arrived and ascended the stand
And then he addressed this remarkable band —
"The contest is on as is shown on the bills
We've precluded the use of injections and pills."

Mrs. Bindle arrived amidst roars of applause
And promptly proceeded to pull down her drawers,
For though she'd no chance in the farting display
She'd the prettiest arse you'd seen in a day.

Now young Mrs. Pothole was backed for a place
Though she'd often been placed in the deepest disgrace
By dropping a fart that had beaten the organ
As well as the vicar, the Reverend Morgan.

The ladies lined up, got the signal to start
And winning the toss Mrs. Jones took first fart.
The people around, in silence and wonder,
Heard the wireless announce gale warnings and thunder.

Now Mrs. McLeod reckoned nothing of this
She'd had some weak tea and was all wind and piss
So she took up her place with her arse open wide
But unluckily shat and was disqualified.

Then young Mrs. Pothole was called to the front
And started by doing a wonderful stunt:
She took a deep breath and clenching her hands
She blew the whole roof off the popular stands.

This left Mrs. Bindle who shyly appeared
And smiled at the clergy who lustily cheered
And though it was reckoned her chances were small
She ran out a winner outfarting them all.

With hands on her hips she stood farting alone
And the crown stood amazed at the sweetness of tone
And the clergy agreed without hindrance or pause
And said "Now, Mrs. Bindle, please pull up your drawers."

With muscles well tensed and legs full apart
She started a full and glorious fart
Beginning with Chopin and ending with swing
She went right up the scale to 'God Save the King'.

She went to the rostrum with maidenly gait
And took from the vicar a set of gold plate
Then she turned to the vicar with sweetness sublime
And smilingly said "Come and see me some time."

FATHER'S GRAVE

They're digging up Father's grave to build a sewer,
    They're digging it up regardless of expense,
They're shifting his remains
    To put in ten inch drains
To take away the shit from residents.

        Gor' Blimey

What's the use of having religion,
    If when you die your troubles never cease,
All because some big nosed twit
    Wants a pipe line for his shit,
Why won't they let the poor guy rest in peace.

        Gor' Blimey

But father all his life was never a quitter
    I don't suppose he'll be a quitter now,
And when the job's complete
    He'll haunt that shit-house seat
And only let them shit when he'll allow.

        Gor' Blimey

Won't there be some fucking consternation,
    And won't those bleeding toffs just rant and rave,
But they'll get what they deserve
    For having the bleeding nerve
To fuck about with a British workman's grave.

THE SECOND OLDEST PROFESSION
(TUNE: Vicar of Bray)

The vicar of the village church to the Curate said for fun,
"I bet I've stuffed more boys than you", the Curate he said,"Done".
"We'll stand outside the village church and this shall be our sign;
You say 'Ding dong' to the boys you've done, I'll say 'Ping pong' to mine",
Ding dong, Ding dong, Ping pong, Ping pong, there were more Ding dongs
                                than there were Ping pongs,
When suddenly a nice boy came along and the Curate said "Ping pong",
Said the vicar "There's no 'Ping pong' there, it is my son I do declare",
"I don't give a bugger 'cos I've been there with a Dinga Dinga Dong Ping pong".

THE GAY CABALLERO

There once was a gay Caballero, an exceedingly gay Caballero,
A flashing the end of Maralta Mari, Malta, Maralta Mari.

He went to a low down casino, an exceedingly low down casino,
And of course he took with him etc., etc.

He there met a fair senorita, an exceedingly fair senorita,
And of course he suggested etc., etc.

He lay her down on a sofita, an exceedingly fair sofita,
And he gave her nine inches etc. etc.

He caught a bad dose of clapita, an exceedingly bad dose of clapita,
Right on the end of etc. etc.

He went to a learned Physiciano, an exceedingly learned Physiciano,
Who cut off the end etc. etc.

And now that my story is ended, all those whom my song has offended,
Can suck what is left etc. etc.

THE HEDGEHOG
(TUNE: Eton Boating Song)

The exhaustive and careful enquiries
Of Darwin and Huxley and Ball
Have conclusively proved that the hedgehog
Can hardly be buggered at all.
But further most painful researches
Have incontrovertibly shown
That this state of comparative safety
Is enjoyed by the hedgehog alone.

The sexual life of the camel
Is stranger than everyone thinks
For at the height of the mating season
He endeavours to bugger the Sphinx.
But the Sphinx's sexual orifice,
Is blocked by the sands of the Nile,
Which accounts for the hump on the camel
And the Sphinx's inscrutable smile.

147

GOOD SHIP VENUS

'Twas on the good ship Venus, by God you should have seen us
The figure head was a whore in bed and the mast a rampant penis.

The skipper of this lugger, his name was Mike McGrugger
He wasn't fit to shovel shit, the fornicating bugger.

The mate his name was Slaughter he fell into the water
He hit his cock upon a rock and now it's two feet shorter.

The bosun's name was Andy by God that man was randy
We filled his bum with boiling rum for pissing in the brandy.

The deckhand's name was Blighted he always got excited
He filled his bunk with shit and spunk whenever land was ighted.

The lookout Mephistophorous he dipped his knob in phosphorus
and stood all night to shine a light to guide us through the Bosphorus.

The ship's dog's name was Rover we turned the bugger over
We ground and ground that poor hound down from Tenerife to Dover.

The skipper's wife was Mabel, whenever she was able
She gave the crew their daily screw upon the chart room table.

The skipper's sister Charlotte a dirty little harlot
First thing at night her twat was white, in the morning it was scarlet.

The skipper's virgin daughter she fell into the water
Ecstatic squeals proclaimed that eels had found her sexual quarter.

The cabin boy a nipper, was a regular Jack the Ripper,
He stuffed his arse with broken glass and circumcised the skipper.

The engineer McSandy by gum that man was randy
He rubbed his prick against a brick and shot a pint of brandy.

The second engineer McCollock who only had one bollock
While trying to float a motor boat he caught it in a rowlock.

The greaser's name was Waring renowned for deeds of daring
His golden rule to insert the tool inside the big end bearing.

The stoker's name was Zember he had a mighty member
He tried to shag some red-hot slag and burned it to an ember.

We had an evil surgeon who didn't need no urgin'
His penis rose and wiped his nose whenever he saw a virgin.

The doctor's name was Lester he was a virgin tester
Through membranes thick he thrust his prick till it began to fester.

We sailed to the Canaries, the crew thought they were fairies;
They caught the syph at Tenerife and clap at Buenos Aires.

We sailed to Nigeria, the crew were getting beerier
The prostitutes along the route grew wearier and wearier.

The mates in the Bahamas wore striped silk pyjamas
The girls thought pricks were wooden sticks not bloody great bananas.

The third engineer was Morgan by God he was a gorgon
He'd entertain the lower deck with tunes upon his organ.

The second mate was Carter my God he was a farter
Upon his ard he played anything from God save the King to Beethoven's
Appassionata

'Twas on the China station for lack of concentration
We sank a junk with loads of spunk by mutual masturbation.

And so to end this serial for want of more material
We'll leave this crew in Timbuctoo in a hospital venereal.

HOW THE MONEY ROLLS IN

My father's an apple pie vendor
    My mother makes synthetic gin,
My sister walks out of an evening,
    And Gosh, how the money rolls in.

CHORUS
Rolls in,   rolls in
My Gosh, how the money rolls in, rolls in
Rolls in, rolls in,
My Gosh, how the money rolls in.

My brother's a keen missionary,
    Wot saves pure young maidens from sin,
He'll save you a blonde for ten dollars.
    Oh Gosh, how the money rolls in.

I'd an uncle who was a night watchman
Who spent all his nights in the pit,
He used to come home in the mornings
All covered all over with shit.

One night was so dark and so stormy,
When uncle went down to the pit,
The wind went and blew out his candle,
And uncle fell down in the shit.

Poor uncle he never recovered,
From this accident down in the pit —
His funeral takes place tomorrow,
He'll be buried in six feet of shit.

IN MOBILE

There's a shortage of good whores, in Mobile,
There's a shortage of good whores, in Mobile,
There's a shortage of good whores, in Mobile,
But there's key-holes in the doors
And there's knot-holes in the floors, in Mobile.

There's a blockage in the bogs, in Mobile (3 times)
It's a habit of the working classes
When they've finished with their glasses
They just stuff them up their arses, in Mobile.

Oh, the old dun cow is dead, in Mobile (3 times)
But the children must be fed
So we'll milk the bull instead, in Mobile.

Oh, the eagles they fly high, in Mobile (3 times)
And they shit right in your eye
So thank God the cows don't fly, in Mobile.

Oh, the negros they grow tall, in Mobile (3 times)
But they shoot 'em in the fall
And they eat 'em balls and all, in Mobile.

Oh, the parson he has come, in Mobile (3 times)
  With his words of Kingdom Come
He can stuff them up his bum, in Mobile.

There's no shortage of good beer, in Mobile (3 times)
  And they give us damn good cheer
Oh, thank God that we are here, in Mobile.

There's a lovely girl called Dinah, in Mobile (3 times)
  For a fuck there is no finer
'Cause she's got the best vagina, in Mobile.

There's a man called Lanky Danny, in Mobile (3 times)
  And his instinct is uncanny
When he's fingering a fanny, in Mobile.

There's a tavern in the town, in Mobile (3 times)
  Where for half a fucking crown
You can get a bit of brown, in Mobile.

Oh, the girls all wear tin pants, in Mobile (3 times)
  But they take them off to dance
Just to give the boys a chance, in Mobile.

There's excess of copulation, in Mobile (3 times)
  They relax for stimulation
On mutual masturbation, in Mobile.

The C.O. is a bugger, in Mobile (3 times)
  And the adj. he is another
So they bugger one another, in Mobile.

A HOUSING PROBLEM

A married couple reviewed a house in the country and on their return remembered that they had not noticed where the W.C. was, so they wrote to the Vicar who had shown them around, asking him if he knew where it was.

Being ignorant of the term 'W.C.', the Vicar thought it meant 'Wesleyan Chapel'. Imagine the surprise of the couple when they received this letter:

'I regret to inform you that the nearest W.C. in your district is 5 miles away from your house. Rather unfortunate if you are in the habit of going regularly.

However, it may interest you to know that many people take their lunch and make a day of it.

By the way, it is built to accommodate 1,000 people and it has been decided to replace the wooden seats by plush ones to ensure greater comfort, especially for people who have to sit a long time before proceedings begin.

Some people go by train, but others who can spare the time walk and get there just in time. I myself never go.

There are special facilities for ladies presided over by the Minister who gives them all the assistance he can.

The children all sit together and sing together during proceedings.

The first time my wife went she had to stand all the time.

Hoping this will be of use to you

Trusting you will attend regularly,
Yours faithfully,

THE VICAR
P.S. Hymn Sheets are to be found behind the door.'

THE KEYHOLE

I left my girl quite early, 'twas barely half past nine,
And by a stroke of bloody good luck her room was next to mine;
Like Christopher Columbus I started to explore,
I took up my position by the keyhole in the door.

CHORUS:
Oh the keyhole, keyhole, keyhole, keyhole, keyhole in the door,
– repeat last line of verse –

My maid sat by the fireside, her dainty toes to warm,
She only had a chemie on to cover her lily white form;
And if she took that chemie off I could not ask for more,
– By Christ, I saw her do it through the keyhole in the door.

At last with trembling fingers I knocked upon the door
And after much persuasion I crossed that threshold floor;
To stop some bastard seeing what I had seen before,
I stuffed that lily white chemie in the keyhole in the door.

That night I spent in glory and other things besides,
And on her heaving bosom had many a joyful ride;
And when I woke next morning John Tom was long and sore,
I felt as though I'd stuffed him through the keyhole in the door.

INSTRUCTIONS TO PASSENGERS
(TUNE: Humoresque)

Passengers will please refrain
From passing water while the train
Is standing in the station, or nearby;
Hoboes riding underneath.
Will get it in their hair and teeth
And they won't like it,
Nor would I.
Whilst the train is in the station
We encourage constipation
A little self control is what we need;
If you really must pass water
Please inform the station porter
Who will place a vessel in the vestibule;
While the train is in the station
We encourage constipation
That is why we have to make this rule.

I TOOK MY WIFE FOR A SCRAMBLE

I took my wife for a ramble, a ramble along a shady lane,
She caught her foot in a bramble, a bramble and arse over bollocks she came.

CHORUS:
Singing,
Ay jig a jig, Ay jig a jig, follow the band,
Follow the band all the way, singing
Ay jig a jig, Ay jig a jig, follow the band,
Fall in and follow the band.

I asked her if she was offended, offended, I asked her if she was in pain,
Before she could answer, could answer, could answer, she was arse over bollocks again.

She'd only one arm in her shimmy, her shimmy, she'd only one leg in her drawer,
She'd only one hair on her titty, her titty, her old man had only one ball.

THE HOLE IN THE ELEPHANT'S BOTTOM

My ambition's to go on the stage and now my ambition I've gotten.
In pantomime I'm all the rage, as the hole in the elephant's bottom.

The manager says, 'It's all balls' but somehow I manage to spot 'em
And wink at the whores in the stalls through the hole in the elephant's bottom.

The manager knows I'm a fool; when the elephant's tail I've forgotten,
But I hang my magnificent tool through the hole in the elephant's bottom.

I'm a lover of beautiful girls: yes ladies I've always been hot on
I turn round and wink at the stuff in the stalls through the hole in the
    elephant's bottom.

My part doesn't have any words so it really cannot be forgotten;
I simply drop property turds through the hole in the elephant's bottom.

Two nancy-boys came in one day, and before anybody could stop 'em
They handed a lovely bouquet through the hole in the elephant's bottom.

The fellow who plays the front part, as an actor is just bloody rotten;
He simply does nothing but fart, and I am the elephant's bottom.

The chorus girls wear *crepe-de-chine* drawers and the sweat makes the fabric go rotten;
When they burst, there are roars of applause from the hole in the elephant's bottom.

Two pockets I've cut in the cloth, for two bottles of beer when I've got 'em
Folks laugh as I blow out the froth through the hole in the elephant's bottom.

There are many more words in this song but I'm sorry to say I've forgot 'em
If you've found this song just a bit too long, you can all kiss the elephant's bottom.

KATHUSALEM

In Jerusalem there lived a maid, a maid who did a roaring trade,
A prostitute of low repute the harlot of Jerusalem.

CHORUS:
Hi, hi Kathusalem, Kathusalem, Kathusalem,
Hi, hi Kathusalem, the harlot of Jerusalem.

This wily maid she had no fear of syphilis or pregnancies,
She kept it clear with gonorrhoea, the pride of all Jerusalem.

There lived a student by a wall, although he'd only got one ball,
He'd been through all or nearly all the harlots of Jerusalem.

One night returning from a spree with customary cockstand he,
Although he'd only got 3 "d" accosted old Kathusalem.

She took the student to a nook, undid his flies and out she took,
His penis shaped just like a hook, the pride of all Jerusalem.

He seized that harlot by the bum, she rattled like a Lewis gun,
He sowed the seed of many a son in the harlot of Jerusalem.

There suddenly loomed up in sight an   Ismaelite, a fucking shite,
For he'd arranged to screw that night the harlot of Jerusalem.

He grabbed that student by the crook, and swearing by the holy book,
He held him o'er the Hebron brook that flows by all Jerusalem.

The student came back full of fight, and grabbed that fucking Ismaelite,
And rammed him up with all his might the arsehole of Kathusalem.

The dirty pro she knew her part, she closed her fan and blew a fart,
And sent the bastard like a dart high above Jerusalem.

Away he soared right out to sea, just like a bloody bumble bee,
And left his bollocks on a tree way up above Jerusalem.

THE KIDNEY WIPER

My lady was a-dressing,
A-dressing for a ball,
When she espied a tinker
Pissing up against the wall.

CHORUS:
With his jolly great kidney wiper
And his balls as big as three
And half a yard of foreskin
Hanging down below his knee;
Hanging down, swinging free,
And half a yard of foreskin
Hanging down below his knee.

My lady wrote a letter
And in it she did say
She'd rather be fucked by a tinker
Than her husband any day.

The tinker got the letter
And when it he did read
His balls began to fester
And his prick began to bleed.

He mounted on his charger
And on it he did ride
His prick slung on his shoulder
And his bollocks by his side.

He fucked the cook in the kitchen
And the housemaid in the hall
" 'Cor Blimey," said the butler
"He's come to fuck us all."

And now that the tinker's dead, sir,
And doubtless gone to hell
He swore he'd fuck the devil
And I'm sure he'd do it well.

LIFE PRESENTS A DISMAL PICTURE
(TUNE: German National Anthem)

Life presents a dismal picture
From the cradle to the tomb
Father's got an anal stricture
Mother's got a fallen womb;
Kate has chronic menstruations
Never laughs nor never smiles
I've got a genial occupation
Cracking ice for Gran-pa's piles.

Little Sue has been aborted
For the forty second time;
Brother William's been deported
To a home for sexual crime;
And the baby's no exception
For his head is full of nits,
Every time he coughs he vomits
Every time he farts he shits.

But we must not be downhearted
We must not be put about
Uncle Jimmy has just farted
And blown his arsehole inside out.

LAST NIGHT
(TUNE: Funiculi, Funicula)

Last night I pulled my pud, it did me good, I knew it would,
                                 I knew it would.
Last night I pulled my pud, it did me good, I knew it would,
                                 I knew it would.
Smash it, bash it, throw it on the floor,
Smite it, bite it, jam it in the door.
Some go in for buggery and some think fucking's good,
But for personal enjoyment I prefer to pull my pud.

LAST SATURDAY NIGHT

When I came home last Saturday night as drunk as I could be
I saw a hat upon the peg where my hat ought to be   (1)
I said to my wife, my darling wife, "I hope you are true to me,
Whose hat is that upon the peg where my hat ought to be?"
She said, "You're drunk you cunt, you silly old cunt
You're as drunk as a cunt can be
For that's a pudding basin your mother gave to me".   (2)
Now all the world I've travelled, ten thousand miles or more
But a basin with a hat-band I've never seen before.   (3)

Substitute the following lines in the above numbered lines:—

1. A coat upon the bed where my coat ought to be
2. For that's a blanket your mother gave to me
3. A blanket with brass buttons on I've never seen before.

1. A head beside the head where my head ought to be
2. For that's a turnip your mother gave to me
3. A turnip with a moustache on I've never seen before.

1. A thing beside the thing where my old thing should be
2. For that's a rolling pin your mother gave to me
3. A rolling pin with bollocks on I've never seen before.

LIMERICKS

There was a young man of Fashoda,
Who wouldn't pay a whore what he owed her,
So she jumped out of bed,
With her cunt flaming red,
And pee'd in his whisky and soda.

There was a young girl of Fashoda
Who lived in a Chinese Pagoda.
The walls and the halls
Were bestrewn with the balls
And the tools of the fools that bestroda.

There was a young man of Bengal,
Who had an octagonal ball,
The square of its weight,
Times the cube root of eight,
Was twice times the root of damn all.

There was a young lady of Leeds.
Who swallowed a packet of seeds,
From out of her arse,
Grew long blades of grass,
And out of her cunt grew weeds.

I am the King of Siam,
For women I care not a damn,
But soft bottomed boys,
Ah! Heavenly joys,
They call me a Bugger — I am.

There was a young girl of Madrid,
Who thought she was having a kid,
So she stuffed it with rubber,
To kill the poor mugger,
And turned out a Goodyear non-skid.

There was a young lady of Ozzit,
Who went to a water closet,
But when she got there,
She could only pass air,
That wasn't a pennyworth was it?

There was a young man of Devizes.
Who was brought up before the Assizes,
For teaching young boys
Matrimonial joys,
And giving them frenchies as prizes.

There was a young man of Madras,
Whose balls were made of brass
In windy weather
They'd clang together,
And sparks would fly out of his arse.

There was a young couple of Aberystwith,
Who united the things they kissed with;
And as they grew older,
They grew so much bolder,
They united the things they pissed with.

The Chippie had been round Cape Horn,
He wished he'd never been born,
He wouldn't have been
If his mother had seen
His father's French letter was torn.

THE MAYOR OF BAYSWATER

The Mayor of Bayswater's
Got a whore for a daughter
And the hairs of her Dickey-di-do
Hang down to her knee.

I know 'cause I've seen 'em
I've been up and in between 'em
The hairs of her Dickey-di-do
Hang down to her knees

One black one, one white one,
And one with a bit of shite on,
The hairs of her Dickey-di-do
Hang down to her knee.

And if I should court her,
I'd have 'em cut shorter,
The hairs of her Dickey-di-do
Hang down to her knees.

MR. CODFISH AND MR. SOLE
(TUNE: Church's One Foundation)

Good morning Mr. Codfish, good morning Mr. Sole,
I tried to fuck your daughter, I couldn't find her 'ole.
At last I found her 'ole sir, just beneath her 'and,
But give me all the world sir, I couldn't raise a stand.

At last I got a stand sir, very long and thin,
But give me all the world sir, I couldn't pop it in.
At last I popped it in sir and waggled it about,
But give me all the world sir, I couldn't get it out.

At last I got it out sir all spunky red and raw,
But give me all the world sir I'll fuck that girl no more.
Oh yes I've learned my lesson that women are no good,
So give me all the world sir, I'll pull my fucking pud.

LYDIA PINK

CHORUS:
We'll drink a drink, a drink, a drink,
To Lydia Pink, a Pink, a Pink,
The saviour of the human race,
She invented a vegetable compound
Efficacious in every case.

Mr. Brown had a very small penis,
And he could hardly raise a stand
So they gave him some of the compound
Now he comes in either hand.

Now Master Brown had very small knackers,
They were just like a couple of peas
So they gave him some of the compound
(Bass) Now they hang below his knees.

Now Mrs. Brown had very small bosoms,
They hardly showed beneath her blouse,
So they gave her some of the compound
And now they milk her, just like the cows.

Mrs. Jones had a very bad stricture
She could hardly bear to pee
So they gave her some of the compound,
Now they pump her direct to the sea.

Mrs. Green was having a baby,
And the pain it was hard to bear
So they gave her some of the compound
And now she's having it over a chair.

Mrs. Black had a very tight grummet,
And she could hardly pee at all
So they gave her some of the compound,
Now she's like Niagara Falls.

LITTLE ANGELINE

She was sweet sixteen, little Angeline
Pure and innocent she'd always been
Never had a thrill and a virgin still,
Poor Little Angeline.

Now the village Squire had a low desire —
The dirtiest bastard in the whole damn shire—
He had his heart on the vital part
Of Poor Little Angeline.

At the village fair the Squire was there,
Masturbating in the local square,
And his tool was raw at the sight
Of Poor Little Angeline.

As she raised her skirt to avoid the dirt
Stepping through the puddle of the Squire's last squirt
He chanced to see the comely knee
Of Poor Little Angeline.

He lifted off his hat and said,"Your cat
Has been run over and it's been crushed quite flat
My car is in the square, can I take you anywhere?"
Poor Little Angeline.

Now the dirty turd should have got the bird
But instead she followed him without a word.
As they drove away you could hear the people say,
"Poor Little Angeline".

They hadn't gone far when he stopped the car
And took her into a low down bar
Where he gave her gin to tempt her into sin,
Poor Little Angeline.

When he'd oiled her well he took her to a dell
Where he'd decided that he'd give her hell
And try his luck with a low down fuck with
Poor Little Angeline.

She cried out "Rape" when he raised her cape;
Poor little girlie there was no escape
It was time someone came to save the maiden's name,
Poor Little Angeline.

But the tale is told of a Blacksmith bold
Who'd loved little Angeline for years untold
And he vowed to be true, whatever they might do
To Poor Little Angeline.

But sad to say that selfsame day
He'd been put to prison for years to stay,
For coming in his pants at the village dance
With Poor Little Angeline.

Now the Blacksmith's cell overlooked the dell
Where the Squire was giving little Angeline hell,
And looking through the bars he recognised the arse
Of Poor Little Angeline.

When he saw them start he blew a might fart
And the walls of the prison simply fell apart
And he ran like shit lest the Squire should split
Poor Little Angeline.

When he got to the spot and saw what was what
He tied the villain's penis in a granny knot,
And as he writhed on his guts, he was kicked in the nuts
By Poor Little Angeline.

Oh Blacksmith true, I love you I do
And I see by your trousers that you love me too
Since I'm undressed come and do your best
For Poor Little Angeline.

Now it won't take long to complete my song
'Cos the hero had a penis one foot long
And his phallic charm was as brawny as his arm —
HAPPY HAPPY ANGELINE.

LADY JANE

It nearly broke her father's heart
When Lady Jane became a tart,
But blood is blood and race is race,
And so to save the family face
He bought her quite the nicest beat
On the shady side of Jermyn Street.

Her father's strict regulations
Regarding all her copulations;
No balls could nestle with her charms
Unless they bore a coat of arms;
No prick could ever hope for entry
Unless it came of landed gentry.

And so her fame began to swell
A vast exclusive clientele.
'Twas even rumoured, without malice,
She had a client at the Palace,
And long before her sun had set
She'd fucked her way right through Debrett.

It hardly took poor father's fancy
When brother Claude became a Nancy.
He thought their friends would all neglect 'em
If common chaps used young Claude's rectum,
So Claude swore he would hawk his steerage
Exclusively among the peerage.

Her Ladyship, abandoning caution,
Then gave classes in abortion.
Her daughter, her first patient, died,
She spent the next ten years inside.
Poor Father, feeling rather limp
Regretfully became a pimp.

THE LOBSTER SONG

Good morning Mr. Fisherman, how do you do,
Have you a lobster you can sell to me?
Yes, sir, said he, I have two,
And the biggest of the bastards I will give to you,

Singing
Roe tiddly oh, Roe tiddly oh, Roe tiddly oh, tiddly oh, toe, toe, toe.

When I got home I couldn't find a dish,
So I put it in the pot where the missis used to piss,

Early next morning the old woman rose,
Up with her nightie and let the waters flow,

At first she gave a scream then she gave a grunt,
And she leapt around the room with the lobster on her cunt,

I grabbed the poker, she grabbed a broom,
We chased the flipping lobster all round the room,

I hit it in the back, hit it in the side,
Hit it in the bollocks till the poor bastard died,

The moral of this story, is very plain to see,
Always have a shuftie before you have a pee,

This is my story, I'll tell you no more,
There's an apple up my arse
And you can have the core.

Singing,
Ro, tiddly oh, oh.

LONG STRONG BLACK PUDDING
Recitational Chorus

A is for A,
A?
L is for Long,
Long? A long.
S is for Strong.
Strong? Long strong. A long strong.
B is for Black.
Black? Strong black. Long strong black. A long strong black.
P is for Pudding.
Pudding? Black pudding. Strong black pudding. Long strong black
    pudding. A long strong black pudding.

*And so on, on the same lines, with each initial of a fresh word,
to the final:*

S is for Sideways.
Sideways? Nightly sideways. Twice nightly sideways. Arsehole
twice nightly sideways. Cat's arsehole twice nightly sideways.
Sister's cat's arsehole twice nightly sideways. My sister's
cat's arsehole twice nightly sideways. Up my sister's cat's
arsehole twice nightly sideways. Pudding up my sister's
cat's arsehole twice nightly sideways. Black pudding up my
sister's cat's arsehole twice nightly sideways. Strong black
pudding up my sister's cat's arsehole twice nightly sideways.
Long strong black pudding up my sister's cat's arsehole twice
nightly sideways....

**A LONG STRONG BLACK PUDDING UP MY SISTER'S
CAT'S ARSEHOLE TWICE NIGHTLY SIDEWAYS'**

THE OLD WOMAN OF DUBLIN

There was an old woman in Dublin did dwell,
And the dirty old bitch I knew her quite well,
She went to the country for a holiday.
She was goosed right and left before she got half way.

CHORUS:
Toor-a-loo, toor-a-lay, it's a bloody fine song
I could sing it all day;
Toor-a-loo, not a bit, it's a bloody fine song
But it's all about shit.

She got up in the night for she wanted the pot
Which perchance the old slave entirely forgot
Said she,"I can't help it if things come to pass",
So she upped wid the winder and stuck out her arse.

A smart young policeman was walking his beat
Which happened to be in that part of the street;
He gazed at the stars as they shone in the sky,
And a bit of soft shit caught him right in the eye.

And this is the trouble that old bitch did cause
The poor young policeman was axed from the force;
And if you go to Dublin you can there see him sit
Wid a card round his neck saying "Blinded by shit".

THE OLD FARMER

There was an old farmer who stood on a rick,
Shouting and swearing and waving his
Fist at the sailors who sat on the rocks
Teaching the children to play with their
Kites and their marbles as in days of yore,
When along came a lady who looked like a
Decent young lady, she walked like a duck,
She said she was teaching a new way to
Educate the children, to sew and to knit,
While the boys in the stables were shovelling the
Contents of the stables, the muck and mud,
The dirty old Squire was pulling his
Horse from the stable to go on a hunt,
His wife in her boudoir was powdering her
Nose and arranging her vanity box,
And taking precautions to ward off the
Gout and rheumatics which left her so stiff,
How well she remembered her last dose of
What did you think I was going to say
You dirty old bastards, that's all for today.

THE RAJAH-SAHIB OF ASTRAKHAN

The Rajah-Sahib of Astrakhan, Yo-ho, Yo-ho,
  A most licentious cunt of a man, Yo-ho, Yo-ho,
Had wives a hundred and forty nine,
  And many a favourite concubine.

CHORUS:
Yo-ho, ye buggers, Yo-ho, ye buggers,
Yo-ho, Yo-ho, Yo-ho.

One night he woke with a hell of a stand, Yo-ho, Yo-ho,
  He called for a warrior, one of his band, Yo-ho, Yo-ho,
You bugger, you cunt, you bastard, you swine,
  Go bring me my favourite concubine.

The warrior brought his concubine, Yo-ho, Yo-ho,
  A face like Venus, a form divine, Yo-ho, Yo-ho,
The Rajah gave a hell of a grunt,
  And shoved his penis up her cunt.

The Rajah's stroke was long and slick, Yo-ho, Yo-ho,
  And soon the maiden was breathing quick, Yo-ho, Yo-ho,
But just as the fuck came to a head,
  The silly buggers fell through the bed.

There's a moral to this tale, Yo-ho, Yo-ho,
  There's a moral to this tale, Yo-ho, Yo-ho,
There's a moral to it all,
  Always fuck 'em against a wall.

OUR OUTSIDE W.C.

Please don't burn our shithouse down,
Mother is willing to pay.
Father's away on the ocean wave,
Kate's in the family way,
Brother dear has gonorrhoea,
Times are fucking hard —
So please don't burn our shithouse down
Or we'll have to shit out in the yard.

THE RAM O' DERBYSHIRE
(TUNE: The Lincolnshire Poacher)

Now in the county of Derbyshire
There was a famous ram.
His fame was spread o'er the countryside
His prick was like a ham.

CHORUS:
And if you don't believe me
And you think I'm telling a lie
Just ask the maids of Derbyshire
Who'll tell you the same as I.

And when the ram was born, Sir,
He had two horns of brass,
One stuck out of his abdomen
The other stuck out of his arse.

And when the ram was young, Sir,
He had a curious trick
Of jumping over a five-barred gate
And landing on his prick.

And when the ram was middle-aged
They carried him in a truck,
And all the maids of Derbyshire
Came down to have a fuck.

And when the ram was old, Sir,
The put him aboard a lugger,
And all the boys of Derbyshire
Came up to have a bugger.

And when the ram was dead, Sir,
They buried him in St. Paul's;
It took ten men and an omnibus
To carry one of his balls.

SAMBO WAS A LAZY COON

Sambo was a lazy coon,
He would sleep in the afternoon,
Under a tree,
So tired was he,
When along came a bee
Making whoopee.
Bzz..Bzz..Bzz..
Get along you bumble bee,
I ain't no rose
I ain't no syphilitic flea,
Get off my flipping nose.
Get off my nasal organ,
Get away from me,
If you want a bit of fanny
You can have my Granny,
But you'll get no arsehole here.

Arsehole rules the Navy,
But there's fuckall in the Branch.

MY RING A-RANG A-ROO

A maiden fair who had never been screwed,
She went to bed with a man half nude.
He took off her clothes, and her cami knicks too,
And played all night with her ring a-rang a-roo.

CHORUS:
Your ring a-rang a-roo, now what is that?
'It's something warm like a pussy cat,
All covered with hair and split in two,
That's what I call my ring a-rang a-roo.'

Her father came and her father said,
"You've gone and lost your maidenhead,
So pack your grip and baggage too,
And earn your living with your Ricky Dan Do."

She went to town a rollicking whore,
She hung a sign outside her door
"Ten dollars down, no less will do
To have a go at my ring a-rang a-roo. "

A policeman knocked upon her door,
"Have you a license to be a whore?"
She said, "No sir, but I'll tell what I'll do
You can come and have a go at my ring a-rang a-roo."

One day there came a son of a bitch,
Who'd got the pox and seven years' itch,
He had the crabs and clinkers too
And he had a go at her ring a-rang a-roo.

The boys all came, the boys all went,
The price came down to fifteen cents,
From sweet sixteen to seventy two
All had a go at that ring a-rang a-roo.

Now nine days passed and they felt sick
And spots appeared upon their pricks.
They vowed that they — oh, never more —
Would whang it up a ruddy little whore.

Then six months passed and they felt well,
All resolutions went to hell.
Met her again, what could they do
But whang it up her ring a-rang a-roo?

Now after all, they're not to blame
For Adam and Eve were just the same.
He chased poor Eve with his big bamboo
And whanged it up her ring a-rang a-roo.

NEMESIS

My days of youth are over
My torch of life burned out,
What used to be my sex appeal
Is now my water spout.

Time was when of its own accord
'Twould proudly from my trousers spring,
But now I've got a full time job
To find the blasted thing.

It used to be amazing
The way it would behave
As early every morning
It stood and watched me shave.

But as old age approaches
It fair gives me the blues
To see it hang its withered head
And watch me clean my shoes.

THE PORTIONS OF A WOMAN
(TUNE: Tangle o' The Isles)

The portion of a woman that appeals to man's depravity
Is fashioned with considerable care,
And what appears to you to be a simple little cavity,
Is really an elaborate affair.

The doctors of distinction have examined these phenomena
In several experimental games,
And made a list of all the things in feminine abdomena
And given them delightful Latin names.

There's the 'Vulva' and 'Vagina' and the dear old 'Perinaeum'
And the 'Hymen' which is found in certain brides,
And lots of little gadgets which you'd love if you could see them,
The 'Clitoris' and several more besides.

Isn't it a pity that when people idly chatter
Of the mysteries to which I've just referred,
That they speak of such a delicate and complicated matter
With such a short and unattractive word.

O'RILEY'S DAUGHTER

As I was sitting by the fire
Drinking O'Riley's rum and water,
When a thought came in my head
I would shag O'Riley's daughter.

CHORUS:
Yippee-I-A, Yippee-I-A,
Yippee-i-A for the one eyed Riley.
Shove it up, stuff it up, Balls and all
Jig-a-jig-a-jig Tres Bon.

Up the stairs and into bed
Quickly cocking my left leg over,
Never a word the maiden said
But laughed like hell when the job was over.

I heard some footsteps on the stairs
Who could it be but the one eyed Riley,
Fucking great pistols in his hands
Looking for the bloke who had shagged his daughter.

I grabbed the pistols from his hands
Pushed his head in a bucket of water,
Stuffed the pistols up his arse
A bloody sight quicker than I shagged his daughter.

Now O'Riley's dead and gone
He will haunt us all no longer.
We took the lid of his coffin off
To mend a hole in the shit house door sir.

PAINFUL POEMS

Uncle Dick and Auntie Mabel
Fainted at the breakfast table
This should be a solemn warning
Not to do it in the morning.

Uncle Ted has much improved
Since he had his balls removed;
Not only has he lost desire
He now sings treble in the choir.

At a party little Dick
Shouted "Someone suck my prick".
Women fainted, strong men shuddered,
Father said "Well I'll be buggared".

Little Francis home from school
Picked up baby by the tool,
Nursie said "Now Master Francis,
Don't spoil baby's fucking chances".

Little Miss Muffet sat on a tuffet
Her knickers all tattered and torn,
It wasn't a spider that sat down beside her
But little Boy Blue with his Horn.

ROEDEAN SCHOOL

We come from Roedean, nice girls are we,
Try to preserve our virginity;
We know the ropes, we've read Marie Stopes,
We come from Roedean School.

And when we hold our little school dance,
We always wear our little short pants;
We like to give the nice boys a chance,
We come from Roedean School.

And when the Vicar he comes to tea,
We put his hand where it shouldn't be;
We give him brandy we make him randy,
We come from Roedean School.

Our old headmistress, she's quite a sport,
She doesn't mind if we don't get caught;
We take precautions, we have our abortions,
We come from Roedean School.

The Gymn Mistress here is a terrible swell,
In the classroom she shows us as clear as a bell;
Her ideas of love stuff, but gives us the rough stuff,
We come from Roedean School.

We have a page boy his name is Dick,
He really has a very small prick;
It's all right for keyholes and little girlies' weeholes,
But no good at Roedean School.

Our head girl her name is Jane,
She only likes it now and again;
And again and again and again and again
And again and again and again.

We have a schoolgirl her name is Nell,
And when she drops 'em, oh how they smell;
She dropped one last Sunday which hung round till Monday,
Polluting our Roedean School.

We lie in our beds a-thinking each night,
How nice it would be to do the thing right.
We've tried all the wheezes with candles and tweezers,
It's no good at Roedean School.

And in conclusion what we expect,
Whether we're single or just a reject;
It's a quiet little nibble without any quibble,
We've been trained at Roedean School.

SALVATION ARMY

SALVATION ARMY! Taking your time from the clock on the church tower opposite —

CHORUS:
To the citadel — QUICK — MARCH!
Come and join us! Come and join us!
Come and join our happy throng!

Sister Anna — You'll carry the banner!
"But I carried it last time."
Well, you'll carry it *this* time, and don't bloody argue!

Sister Cox — YOU'LL carry the box!
"But I carried it last night."
Well you'll carry it tonight, tomorrow night, and every *other* bloody night!

Sister Tucker — YOU'LL carry the other blighter!
"But I'm in the family way!"
You're in every *bastard's* way!

Sister Nellie — You've got a hole in your belly!
"Well, so would you if you carried the *banner* for *forty flaming years.*"

"I am an ex-naval officer. I used to stand on street corners, and associate with the *wrong kind* of *women.* But now I have seen the *LIGHT:* I have reformed! I feel so happy I could put my foot right through that *BLOODY DRUM!*

Down our street we had a merry party,
Everybody was there all so gay and hearty.
Talk about a treat, we ate all the meat,
And we drank all the beer from the boozer down the street.

There was old Uncle Joe, he was fair fucked up,
So we put him in the cellar with the old bull pup;
Little Sonny Jim was trying to get it in,
With his arse-hole winking at the moon.

Oh, Salome, Salome, that's my girl, Salome,
Standing there with her arse all bare,
Waiting for someone to slide in there,
Oh, slide it, and glide it,
Right up her fucking chute,
Two brass balls with the shankers too
And a foreskin full of shit.

She's a big fat cow, twice the size of me,
She's got hairs on her belly like the branches of a tree,
She can run, jump, fight, fuck,
Wheel a barrow, push a truck,
That's my girl Salome.

On Monday night she takes it up the back,
On Tuesday night she hauls in all the slack,
On Wednesday night she has a spell,
On Thursday night she fucks like hell,
On Friday she takes it up her nose,
In between her fingers, down between her toes,
On Saturday night she dishes out gams,
And she goes to church on Sunday.

I just want to be a Sunbeam,
And a fucking fine Sunbeam am I — Sunbeam am I.

SISTER LILY
(TUNE: The Road to the Isles)

Have you met my Uncle Hector
He's a cock and ball inspector
At a celebrated English Public School
And my brother sells French Letters
And a patent cure for wetters
We're not the best of families — ain't it cruel.

My little sister Lily is a whore in Piccadilly
My mother is another in the Strand.
My 'father hawks his asshole
At the Elephant and Castle
We're the finest fucking family in the land.

SHE WAS POOR BUT SHE WAS HONEST

She was poor but she was honest,
Victim of a Squire's whim.
First he kissed her, then he upped her
And she had a child by him.

It's the same the whole world over
It's the poor wot gets the blame,
It's the rich wot gets the pleasure
Ain't it all a bleedin' shame.

So she ran away to London
For to 'ide 'er grief and shame,
There she met another squire
And she lost her name again.

See 'er ridin' in her carriage
In the park so bright and gay,
Where the nibs and nobby persons
Come to pass the time of day.

There's a cottage in the country
Where 'er poor old parents live,
Drinking champagne wot she sends 'em
But they never can forgive.

In a banker's arms she flutters
Like a bird wot's broke a wing.
First 'e loved 'er then 'e left 'er.
Still she 'asn't got a ring.

See 'im in 'is splendid mansion
Entertainin' with the best,
While the girl wot 'e 'as ruined
Entertains a payin' guest.

See 'im in the 'Ouse of Commons
Making laws to put down crime,
While the victim of 'is passions
Walks the streets midst mud and slime.

See 'im drivin' to the races
To the Ascot Gold Cup 'unt,
Whilst the girl wot 'e disgraces
Earns a livin' through 'er cunt.

See 'er standin' in the gutter
Sellin' matches by the box.
Any man wot tries to up 'er
Is bound to get a dose of pox.

Standin' on the bridge at midnight
Throwin' snowballs at the moon
She said,"Jack I've never 'ad it",
But she spoke too fuckin' soon.

Standin' on the bridge at midnight
Pickin' clinkers from 'er crutch,
She said,"Jack, I've never 'ad it"
He said,"No, not fuckin' much".

SAMMY HALL

Oh, my name is Sammy Hall, Sammy Hall,
Oh, my name is Sammy Hall, Sammy Hall,
Oh, my name is Sammy Hall, and I've only got one ball,
But it's better than fuck-all,

CHORUS:
Damn your eyes, Blast your soul, Bloody Hell, Shit.

Oh, they say I killed a man, killed a man,
Oh, they say I killed a man, killed a man,
For I hit him on the head, with a fucking great lump of lead,
And now the bastard's dead,

And they say I'm to be hung, to be hung,
And they say I'm to be hung, to be hung,
And they say I'm to be hung, for a crime I've never done,
They can stick it up their bum,

So the Sheriff he will come, he will come,
So the Sheriff he will come, he will come,
So the Sheriff he will come, with his finger up his bum,
'Cause he cannot get his thumb,

And the Jury they'll come too, they'll come too,
And the Jury they'll come too, they'll come too,
And the Jury they'll come too, in their nice new suits of blue,
'Cause they've got fuck-all else to do,

Then the parson he will come, he will come,
Then the parson he will come, he will come,
Then the parson he will come, though he looks so fucking glum,
With his tales of Kingdom Come,

And now they're hanging me, hanging me,
And now they're hanging me, hanging me,
And now they're hanging me, Oh ! Someone set me free,
This suspense is killing me,

And now I am in Hell, am in Hell,
And now I am in Hell, am in Hell,
And now I am in Hell, but it's all a fucking sell,
'Cause the parson's here as well,
Damn his eyes, Blast his soul, Bloody Hell, Shit!

SWEET VIOLETS

A matelot told me before he died —
And I have no reason to think he lied —
That his wife had a cunt so wide
That she could never be satisfied.

So he built her a tool of steel,
Driven by a bloody great wheel;
Balls of brass he filled with cream,
And the whole fucking issue was driven by steam.

Round and round went the bloody great wheel,
In and out went the prick of steel,
Till in ecstasy she cried,
"Enough, enough, I'm satisfied".

Now we come to the bitter bit:
There was no means of stopping it
And she was split from arse to tit
And the whole fucking issue was covered with shit.

Sweet violets, sweeter than all the roses,
Covered all over from head to tit,
Covered all over in — Sweet Violets.

THEY CALLED THE BASTARD STEPHEN

A maiden sat in a mountain glen,
Seducing herself with a fountain pen,
The capsule broke and the ink went wild,
And now she's the mother of a blue-black child.

And they called the bastard Stephens,
And they called the bastard Stephens,
And they called the bastard Stephens,
'Cos that was the name of the ink.

No matter how, nor where, nor when,
Use Stephens Ink in your fountain pen.

THAT LOVELY WEEKEND

Thank you so much for that lovely weekend,
Those two nights in bed dear you helped me to spend.
The smile on your face as you tickled my fan,
The thrill that you gave me as you only can.
I lay on the bed dear you played with my breast,
And asked me my darling to take off my vest.
My two lovely bosoms with lovely brown tips,
My two slender legs squeezing right round your hips.
The time was so short dear and you had to go,
You didn't have much time to stay.
Your two balls were drumming, I thought you were coming,
Sorry I cried, but I just felt that way.

And when it was over you dropped off to sleep,
I lifted your shirt dear to just take a peep.
And there was poor Jimmy as small as a shrimp,
Between your legs hanging so wet and so limp.
To mark the occasion we put down the date,
We should have used Rendells but now it's too late,
So please get a licence and marry me soon,
Our child will be born on the 18th of June.

THOSE FOOLISH THINGS

A book of sex with fifty well thumbed pages
An old French letter, that has been used for ages
Abortions quite a few
These foolish Things, remind me of you.

Remember Dear, that we talked of marriage
That was the night you had your first miscarriage
Abortions quite a few
These Foolish Things, remind me of you.

I came, you came, all over me
And in our ecstasy we simply knew that it had to be.

The newsboys calling out "late night final"
The faint aroma of a gents urinal
Oh how the memory clings
These Foolish Things, remind me of you.

The limp inertness of a used French Letter
That I discarded when I knew you better
A bed of creaking springs
These Foolish Things, remind me of you.

I came, you came, all over me,
And in our ecstasy we simply knew that it had to be.

The lumpy sofa that we had our shags on
The smell that told me that you had your rags on
Oh how the memory clings
These Foolish Things, remind me of you.

THE WALRUS AND THE CARPENTER

If forty whores in purple dresses,
Came walking down the Strand,
Do you suppose the Walrus said,
A chap could raise a stand,
I doubt it said the carpenter,
But wouldn't it be grand,
And all the time,
The dirty swine was coming in his hand.

THE WOODPECKER SONG

I put my finger in the woodpecker's hole,
The woodpecker said "God Bless my Soul,
Take it out, take it out, take it out ... Remove it."

Put it back ...   Replace it
Turn it round ...   Revolve it
The other way ...   Reverse it
Slow it down ...   Retard it
Speed it up ...   Increase it
In and out ...   Reciprocate it.

THREE OLD LADIES

Oh dear what can the matter be, three old ladies locked in the lavatory,
They were there from Monday to Saturday,
Nobody knew they were there.

They'd all been to tea with the Vicar,
They went in together because it was quicker,
The lock on the door was a bit of a sticker,
Nobody knew they were there.

The first lady's name was Elizabeth Porter,
She was the Bishop of Chichester's daughter,
She only went there to get rid of some water,
Nobody knew they were there.

The second one's name was Amelia Spender,
She went there to adjust her suspender,
She got it caught up with her feminine gender,
Nobody knew they were there.

The third lady's name was Emily Humphrey,
She stayed there because it was comfy,
She went to get up but could not get her bum free,
Nobody knew they were there.

The fourth one's name was Celia Caution,
She went in to have an abortion,
It came away in a fucking great portion,
Nobody knew they were there.

The fifth one's name was Ermintrude Buntin,
She sat there a-fartin' and gruntin',
The attendant came in and kicked her old cunt in,
Nobody knew they were there.

The sixth lady's name was Felicity Petter,
She went there to try a French letter,
When she got there she found Rendell's were better.
Nobody knew they were there.

WEST VIRGINIAN HILLS

In the hills of West Virginy lived a girl called Nancy Brown,
For beauty and for virtue she was of great renown.
There came the village Deacon to Nancy one fine day,
Took Nancy to the mountains but Nancy wouldn't play.
She came rollin' down the mountain, rollin' down the mountain,
She came rollin' down the mountain might wise,
For she didn't give the Deacon that there thing that he was seekin'
She remained as pure as the West Virginy skies.

There came a roving cowboy with laughter and with song,
Took Nancy to the mountain, but she still knew right from wrong.
She came rollin' down the mountain, rollin' down the mountain,
She came rollin' down the mountain mighty wise,
'Cause despite the cowboy's urgin' she remained the village virgin,
She remained as pure as the West Virginy skies.

Then came Henderson, the trapper, with his phrases sweet and low,
Took Nancy to the mountain, but she still knew "Yes" from "No",
She came rollin' down the mountain, rollin' down the mountain,
She came rollin' down the mountain mighty wise.
She remained, as I have stated, quite uncontaminated,
She remained as pure as the West Virginy skies.

Then came a city slicker with his hundred dollar bills,
Put Nancy in his Packard, and drove her to the hills,
And she stayed up in the mountain, stayed up in the mountain,
Yes, she stayed up in the mountain all night long,
She returned next morning early more a woman than a girlie,
And her mother kicked the hussy out of town.

Now she's living in the city, she's living in the city,
And by all accounts she's living mighty swell.
'Cause she's wining and she's dining
And she's on her back reclining
And the West Virginy skies can go to hell.

Then came ole man Depression, kicked the slicker in the pants,
He had to sell his Packard, and he had to give up Nance,
So she's gone back to the mountains, gone back to the mountains,
Yes, she's gone back to the mountains as of yore.
Now the cowboy and the Deacon
They both get what they were seekin'
For she's just another West Virginy whore.

THE SPARRER

There was a bleedin' sparrer lived up a bleedin' spout,
Then comes a bleedin' rainstorm wot washed the bleeder out.
That bleedin' little sparrer went and sat out on the grass
And told that bleedin' rainstorm to kiss 'is bleedin' arse.
And when that storm was over, and likewise too the rain,
That bleedin' little sparrer flies off up that spout again.
'E builds 'isself a bleedin' nest and lays a bleedin' egg;
The bleeder bursts inside 'is guts and trickles dahn 'is leg.
Then there comes a bleedin' sparrer'awk what spies 'im in 'is snuggery,
'E sharpens up 'is bleedin' claws and chews 'im up to buggery.
Then there comes a bleedin' sportin' cove wot 'as a bleedin' gun;
'E shot that bleedin' sparrer'awk and spoilt 'is bleedin' fun.
Now the moral of my story is plain enough to all —
It's: THEM WOT LIVES UP BLEEDIN' SPOUTS DON'T GET NO
                                          FUN AT ALL.

THE VIRGIN STURGEON

Caviar comes from the virgin sturgeon
The virgin sturgeon's a very fine fish.
The virgin sturgeon needs no urgin'
That's why caviar is my dish.

Shad roe comes from the scarlet shad fish
Shad fish have a sorry fate.
Pregnant shad fish is a sad fish
Got that way without a mate.

Oysters they are fishy bivalves
They have youngsters in their shell.
How they diddle, is a riddle
But they diddle — sure as hell.

The green sea turtle's mate is happy
With her lover's winning ways.
First he grips her with his flippers
Then he grips and flips for days.

Mrs. Clam is optimistic
Shoots her eggs out in the sea
Hopes her suitor is a shooter
Hits the self same spot as she.

Give a thought to happy cod fish
Always there when duty calls
Female cod fish is an odd fish
From them too come codfish balls.

The trout is just a little salmon
Just half grown and minus scales,
But the trout just like the salmon
Can't get on without its tail.

Lucky fishes are the ray-fish
When for youngsters they essay
Yes, my hearties, they have parties
In the good old fashioned way.

I fed caviar to my girl friend
She was a virgin tried and true
Now my virgin needs no urgin'
There ain't nothing she won't do.

I fed caviar to my Grandpa
Grandpa he is 93
Shrieks of laughter heard from Grandma
Grandpa'd had her up a tree.

Fed some caviar to my Grandma
She came down from out that tree.
Now my Grandma and my Grandpa
Start to raise a family.

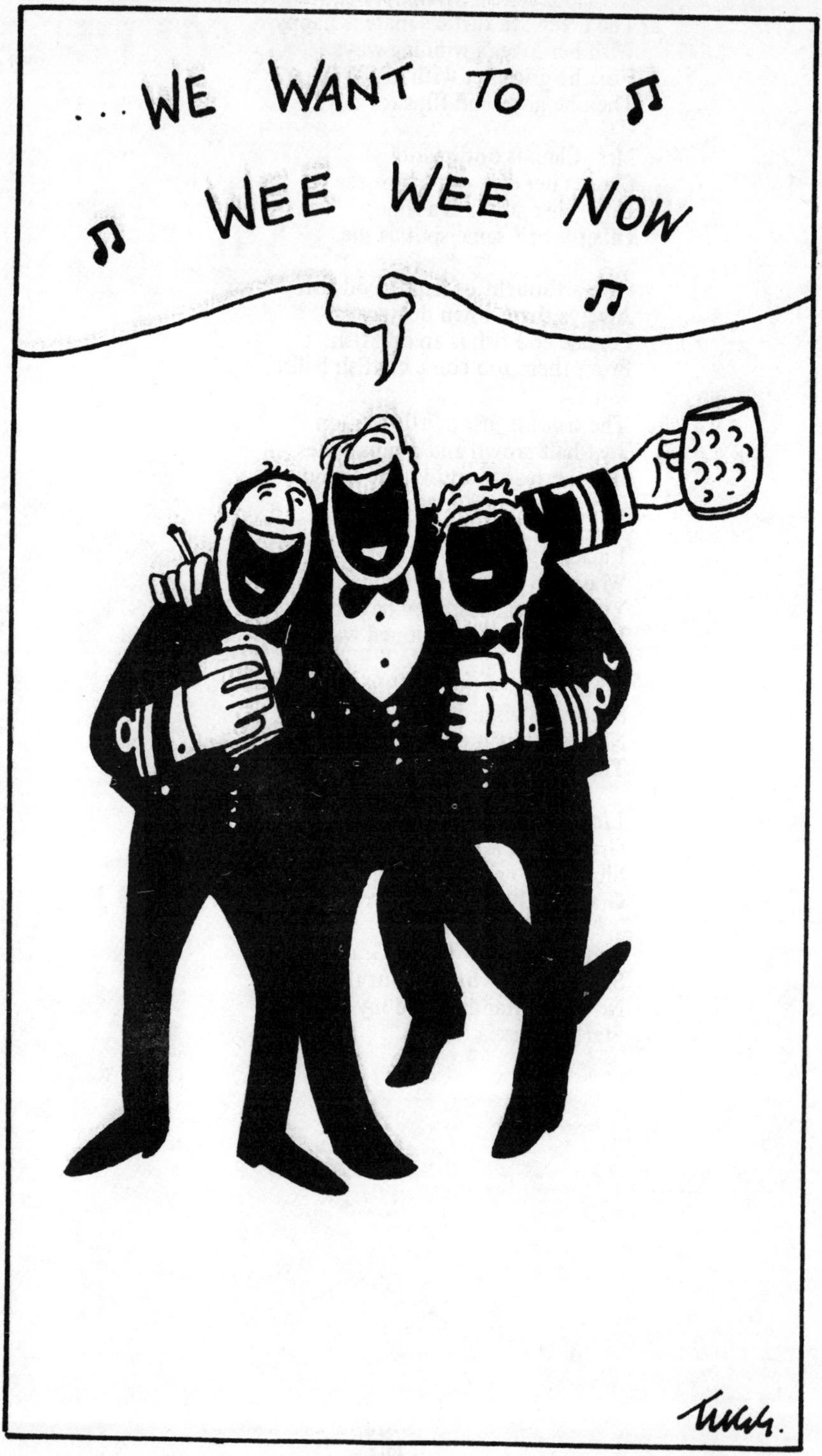
... WE WANT TO
WEE WEE NOW

NAVAL ODES AND DITTIES

HERE BEGINNETH THE LESSON

*The lesson today is taken from the Fifth Book of Guinness,
Second Sunday after Soap and Tobacco Issue.*

And it came to pass that a certain Mess Caterer gathered
unto himself all the Mess Savings and did journey from
Chatchuam, nigh unto Gillinguam, yea, even unto Portsmouthlem.

And he was set upon by thieves; not ordinary thieves, but
arse-thieves, who ragged him, de-bagged him and shagged him,
drew lots for his burberry, and sent him on his way sore but
rejoicing.

And it came to pass that in Portsmouthlem he did come
to the house of an harlot, and he sayeth unto her, 'How much
to tarry the night with thee?' And she did make reply, saying,
'One kitbag, one shitbag, and thirty pieces of silver – Jack!'

And in the morning he did arise and say unto her: 'What
hour is it?' And she, removing a brick from the wall and espying
the Town Hall Clock, did answer, 'It draweth nigh unto noon.'
Whereupon he cried out, 'Lo! I am adrift, even to fuck!'

And he did make way to the Gate called Main, and even
unto No.1 Railway Jetty, where he did espy on the gangway
afar off not a big man, not a small man, not even a gentleman,
but a fucking great Jaunty, and he did fall upon his neck,
breaking it, saying 'Forgive me, Master, for I know not what
I do.'

And he was cast down below, but on the morrow awoke, and
and when he awoke he did squeeze, and he squoze, and a bubble
arose. And, calling for the Marine sentry, he did say, 'Take
thou me to the Apothecary, for I am fucking rotten.'

And he did go before the Apothecary who did order
him to squeeze again. Whereupon he squoze again, and lo, yet
another bubble. And the Apothecary did say, 'Woe unto thee,
for they days are numbered, and henceforth thy knife, fork,
and fucking spoon Jack!

Here endeth the lesson

ALL THE NICE GIRLS
(TUNE: "All The Nice Girls Love A Sailor.")

All the nice girls love a candle,
All the nice girls love a wick,
For there's something about a candle,
That reminds them of a prick:
Bright and breezy, slips in easy,
It's the ladies' pride and joy,
Oh, it's been up Auntie Jane
And it's going up again,
Ship ahoy!
Jack's the boy!

ME NO LIKEE BLITISH SAILOR

Me no likee Blitish sailor,
Yankee sailor come ashore.
Me no likee Blitish sailor
Yankee sailor pay one dollar more.

Yankee sailor call me 'Honey darling',
Blitish sailor call me 'Fucking whore'.
Me no likee Blitish sailor,
Yankee sailor won't you come ashore?

Yankee sailor always were Flench letter,
Blitish sailor never wear fuck-all.
Me no likee Blitish sailor,
Yankee sailor won't you come ashore?

Yankee sailor have one fuck and finish,
Blitish sailor fuck for evermore.
Me no likee Blitish sailor,
Yankee sailor won't you come ashore?

BOLLOCKY BILL THE SAILOR

"Who's that knocking at my door,
Who's that knocking at my door,
Who's that knocking at my door" said the fair young maiden.

"It's only me from over the sea" said Bollocky Bill the sailor.

*(Continue three times for each verse of the maiden and once
each for Bollocky Bill)*

Maiden: I'll come down and let you in.
Bill: And where am I going to sleep tonight.
Maiden: You may sleep upon the mat.
Bill: Oh, Bugger the mat, I can't sleep on that.
Maiden: You can sleep between my thighs.
Bil: What have you got between your thighs.
Maiden: I've got a pin cushion.
Bill: I've got a pin I will stick it in.
Maiden: But what if there should be a child.
Bill: strangle the bastard as soon as it's born.
Maiden: But what about the Police Force.
Bill: Bugger the Police and fuck the Force.
Maiden: But what if there should be an inquest
Bill: Stuff the inquest up your arse.
Maiden: When shall I see you again.
Bill: Never no more you fucking old whore.

SCAPA FLOW
(TUNE: A Little Bit of Heaven")

Sure a little bit of dirt and shit fell out the sky one day,
And it landed in the hogwash not so many miles away;
And when the Navy found it sure it looked so bleak and bare,
They said suppose we leave it for a Naval base up there.
So they dotted it with battleships to make its lakes look grand,
And they crowded it with matelots, the best in all the land;
Then they sprinkled it with rain and sleet and hail and bloody snow,
And when they had it finished sure they called it SCAPA FLOW.

191

DO YOUR BALLS HANG LOW?

(TUNE: Sailors' Hornpipe)

Tiddly winks young man, get a woman if you can,
If you can't get a woman get a clean old man.
From the lofty heights of Malta to the shores of old Gibraltar
Can you do the double shuffle with your balls in a can?

Do your balls hang low, can you swing 'em to and fro?
Can you tie 'em in a knot, can you tie 'em in a bow?
Can you swing 'em o'er your shoulder like a European soldier?
Can you do a double shuffle, do your balls hang low?

Do your balls hang tight, can you hide 'em in a fight?
Can you tuck 'em 'neath your arm, can you keep 'em out of sight?
Are they tough enough to buckle up another man's hard knuckles?
Can you do a double shuffle, do your balls hang tight?

Do your balls hang loose, as loose as a goose?
Can you slide 'em down the hall, can you bounce 'em off the wall?
Does it really make you stammer when you hit 'em with a hammer?
Can you do a double shuffle, do your balls hang loose?

Do your balls hang down, way down to the ground?
Can you slide 'em on the ice, can you crack 'em in a vice?
Does it make your breath come quick when you stick 'em with a pick?
Can you do a double shuffle when your balls hang down?

ROUND THE CORNER

I paid a quid to see
That much tattooed lady:
And right across her jaw
Was the badge of the Anzac Corps,
And on her chest was a possum
With the gay red white and blue,
And on her back was the Union Jack
And a ruddy great Kangaroo.
The map of Germany was where it ought to be,
And right across her hips
Was a line of battleships;
And on her kidney, her kidney,
Was a bird's eye view of Sydney,
And round the corner, round the corner,
Was the (w)hole of Tennessee.

OLD KING COLE

Now Old King Cole was a merry old soul
And a merry old soul was he;
He called for his pipe and he called for a light
And he called for his fiddlers three.

Now every fiddler had a very fine fiddle
And a very fine fiddle had he;
Fiddle-diddle-dee, diddle-dee, said the fiddlers,
Very merry men are we,
There's none so rare as can compare
With the boys of the Queen's Navy.

Now Old King Cole was a merry old soul
And a merry old soul was he;
He called for his pipe and he called for a light
And he called for his painters three.

Now every painter had a very fine brush
And a very fine brush had he;
Slap it up and down, up and down, said the painters
Fiddle-diddle-dee, diddle-dee, said the fiddlers
Very merry men ... etc.

Now Old King Cole was a merry old soul
And a merry old soul was he;
He called for his pipe and he called for a light
And he called for his Tailors three.

Now every tailor had a very fine needle
And a very fine needle had he;
Whip it in and out, in and out, said the tailors,
Slap it up and down, up and down, said the painters,
Fiddle-diddle-dee, diddle-dee, said the fiddlers
Very merry men ... etc.

Now Old King Cole was a merry old soul
And a merry old soul was he;
He called for his pipe and he called for a light
And he called for his Butchers three.

Now every butcher had a very fine block
And a very fine block had he;
Put your meat on the block, said the butchers,
Whip it in and out, in and out, said the tailors,
Slap it up and down, up and down, said the painters,
Fiddle-diddle-dee, diddle-dee, said the fiddlers,
Very merry men ... etc.

Now Old King Cole was a merry old soul
And a merry old soul was he;
He called for his pipe and he called for a light
And he called for his Jugglers three.

Now every juggler had some very fine balls,
And some very fine balls had he.
Throw your balls in the air, said the jugglers,
Put your meat on the block, said the butchers,
Whip it in and out, in and out, said the tailors,
Slap it up and down, up and down, said the painters,
Fiddle-diddle-dee, diddle-dee, said the fiddlers,
Very merry men ... etc.

Now Old King Cole was a merry old soul
And a merry old soul was he;
He called for his pipe and he called for a light
And he called for his coachmen three.

Now every coachman had a very fine horn,
And a very fine horn had he.
I've got the horn, got the horn, said the coachmen,
Throw your balls in the air, said the jugglers,
Put your meat on the block, said the butchers,
Whip it in and out, in and out, said the tailors,
Slap it up and down, up and down, said the painters,
Fiddle-diddle-dee, diddle-dee, said the fiddlers,
Very merry men are we,
There's none so rare as can compare
With the boys of the Queen's Navy.

STRIPEY'S LAMENT

I was wandering through the Dockyard in a panic,
When I met a Stripey old and grey,
He was carrying his kit-bag and his hammick,
And it make me sad to hear him say:
'Oh, I wonder, oh I wonder,
Did the Jaunty make a blunder,
When he made this Draft-chit out for me?
For me...... ?
For I've been a barrack stanchion,
And I've lived in Jago's mansion,
And I always said "Good morning" to the Chief.'

Shout
Good Morning, Chief,
Reply
Fuck orf.!

THE PLUMBERS' RUN

Come across the Seven Seas,
One fat, one thin, one tall,
A Sub. and two Lieutenant (E)s
— Jolly plumbers all.

As of old the bold marauder went to loot the Spanish main,
See them creep across the border to the northward into Spain.

In the dust the dogs lie dreaming, and the frontier stands unbarred,
Guarded by the bayonets gleaming of the sullen Civil Guard.

Through the crowds of whining, pawing beggars, guides, disfigured, lame,
Savagely their progress boring, our gallant heroes came.

Now ho! the night before them stretches, all are in a festive mood.
Sudden pangs — the stomach fetches, first desire of all is food.

Shall we take some small tomatoes, stuffed crustacea at the boil,
Garlic scented new potatoes, or a black cat fried in oil?

Prawns as red as Russia's flag, Sir, — fling away the empty tins,
Eat the entrails of a stag, Sir, to the tune of mandolins.

Anchovies curled like mermaids sleeping, Spanish omelette served with beans,
The souls of long dead sailors creeping in the eyes of tinned sardines.

At last the feast is done and ended, sucking foul and long cigars,
The three their wicked way have wended seeking wenches, wine, guitars.

Now over all the traces kicked, away down Gib. Street, high and wide, ·
The younger has his pocket picked by the snivelling Spanish guide.

Behold the elder, lazy loafer, ogled by a gang of sluts,
Lying back upon a sofa trickling sherry down his guts.

The Sub who's bred on English beer, introduced to wine and harlots
Finds he can neither steam nor steer the erstwhile terror of Queen Charlottes.

See the moon has risen high like a shapely maiden's mouth.
Hear the distant murmuring sigh — 'tis our comrades moving South.

Singing, shouting, banging shutters, wine and blood on coat and cuffs,
Bouncing in the dirty gutters — a revolting crowd of roughs.

Remembering the food he gobbled, feels the creeping hand of Fate,
The fat one's sick upon the cobbles long before they reach the gate.

For taxi-cabs they soon start roaring, deep into their pockets delve,
Slumped across the back seat, snoring, all return at half past twelve.

Nearly falling in the water, calling vainly on the Lord,
Like three Vikings from the slaughter the slobbering drunkards crawl on board.

But see who's padding into sight, like a cat upon a wall,
Or the wolf that comes by night, a stooping figure, lean and tall.

Steaming like a shadowing cruiser, keeping just four cables clear,
Another plumber, late night boozer? — My God! The Senior Engineer!

So be warned, if melancholy, when you hear the sunset gun,
Don't be tempted to the folly of a drunken Plumbers' Run.

COLD AS A FROG
Recitation

Way up in those frozen Arctic regions,
Where you pongoes have never been,
Lie the bones of many a matelot
And many a Royal Marine.
We had no horses to pull our guns,
We had to pull our own cow — sons,
And was it cold?
Cold,
Cold as a frog in an ice-bound pool.
Cold as the tip of an Eskimo's tool.
Cold as the hairs on a Polar bear's chuff.
Cold as the cuss' on a Pusser's duff.
Cold as Charity —
And that's mighty chilly,
But not so cold as our poor Willie.
He's dead,
Fuck his luck,
Off caps,
Poor bastard.
Cold, fucking cold!

SEVEN WHORES OF POMPEY

There were seven whores of Pompey,
A-sipping of their wine,
And the subject for discussion was was
"Is your thing bigger than mine?"
Now up spoke Bloody Mary, her cunt as big as hell,
And in it was a lighthouse and a battleship as well.

CHORUS: *She had those dark and dreamy eyes*
               And a whizzbang up her jacksie, (Taxi!)
               She was one of those flash eyed whores,
               One of the old brigade.

Now the next one was a sailor's wife and she was dressed in blue
And in one corner of her funny little thing she stowed a seaboat's crew,
She stowed a seaboat's crew my boys the rowlocks and the oars,
And in the other corner the Marines were forming fours.

Now the next one was a fisherman's wife and she was dressed in green,
And in one corner of her funny little thing she stowed a soup tureen,
She stowed a soup tureen my boys the ladles and the soup,
And in the other corner Naval Airmen looped the loop.

Now the next one was a brewer's wife and she was dressed in grey.
And in one corner of her funny little thing she stowed a brewer's dray,
She stowed a brewer's dray my boys the barrels and the beer,
And in the other corner she had Syph. and Gonorrhoea.

The next one was a Pongo's wife and she was dressed in red,
And in one corner of her funny little thing she stowed a horse's head,
She stowed a horse's head my boys the bridles and the bit,
And in the other corner Naval airmen shovelling shit.

Now the next one was a C.P.O.'s wife and she was dressed in puce,
And in one corner of her funny little thing she practised self-abuse,
She practised self-abuse my boys in forty different ways,
And in the other corner was Willmott buggering Hayes.

Now the next one was a cricketer's wife and she was dressed in vermilion,
And in one corner of her funny little thing she stowed the Lord's pavilion,
She stowed the Lord's pavilion boys the batsman and his duck,
And in the other corner the remains of last night's fuck.

Now the next one was the Captains wife and she was dressed in gold,
And in one corner of her funny little thing she had the 'Leopold.'
She had the 'Leopold' my boys, the diesels and the oil,
And in the other corner she'd a fucking 'normous boil'.

Then up there spake the airman's wife and she was dressed in beige
And in one corner of her funny little thing she had a Handley Page,
She had a Handley Page my boys with joystick and its knob
And in the other corner were two Naval airmen on the job.

Then up there spake the actor's wife who was also dressed in beige
And in one corner of her funny little thing she had the Windmill stage,
She had the Windmill stage my boys the gallery and stalls
And in the other corner she had C.B. Cochrane's balls.

Then up there spake the observer's wife and she was dressed in chrome
And in one corner of her funny little thing she had the aerodrome,
She had the aerodrome my boys the bombers and the troops
And in the other corner there were Barras Looping loops.

And then there was the ops room girl — she was a little WAAF
And in one corner of her funny little thing she had the ops room staff,
She had the ops room staff my boys all fucking there like hell
And in the other corner she had signals staff as well.

And then up spake the telephone girl and she was dressed very strange
And in one corner of her funny little thing she had the camp exchange,
She had the camp exchange my boys the wire and all the switches
And in the other corner Little F had left his breeches.

And last there spake the Lieutenant's wife and she was dressed so poor
And in her palmy days my boys she'd been a Pompey whore
She'd been a Pompey whore my boys and her price was half a crown,
But now that she's got married her price is coming down.

FRAGMENT FROM THE MED

My name is Venal Vera,
I'm a lovely from Gezira,
And the Fuhrer pays me well for what I do,
And the news of next week's battle
I obtained from last night's rattle
On the golf course with a brigadier from Kew.

1. Have you heard about the big strong man,
   Who lived in a caravan.
   Have you heard about the Jeffrey-Johnson fight,
   When the big buck nigger frought the white.
   I'll take every heavyweight you've got,
   He's the man who'll beat the whole darn lot,
   He used to play the organ in the belfry
   Now he wants to fight Jack Dempsey,

CHORUS
   That's my brother, Sylveste (What has he got?)
   He's got a row of forty medals on his chest (Big Chest)
   He killed forty niggers in the West-he takes no rest,
   Bigga da man — mighty strong — forty inches cross the chest —
   hells fire — son of a gun — stand back — don't push — tons of
   room for you and me,
   He's got an arm — like a leg — lady's leg,
   A punch that would sink a battleship (Big ship)
   It takes all the Army and the Air Force
   To put the wind up — Sylveste.

2. Now he thought he'd take a trip to Italy,
   He thought he'd take a trip by the sea.
   So he dived in the harbour at New York,
   And swam like a man made of cork
   He saw the Lusitania in distress (What did he do?)
   He swallowed all the water in the sea (Big swallow)
   Put the big ship "Lusi" on his chest,
   And took the whole darn lot to Italy.

3. Now he thought he'd take a trip to Old Japan,
   And they turned out the whole brass band.
   He played every instrument they'd got,
   And he mucked up the whole darn lot
   Now all church bells were ringing,
   And all church choirs were singing
   And they all turned one to see — Who?
   My Big, Big, Brother — Sylveste.

SHILLING A GO
(TUNE: *Three Men went to Mow*)

Down in Drury Lane there are some filthy women,
You can get a bit of you know what all for a shilling.
Soldiers half a crown, sailors half a guinea,
Ordinary men two pounds ten schoolboys all a penny.

CHORUS:
Three whores walk the streets always bloody willing,
It's only a bob for a bit of knob all for a shilling.

In the Shetland Isles there are no filthy women,
You can take a leap at any old sheep all for a shilling,
NCOs two, airmen one and sixpence,
You can have a screw on the old black ewe all for a shilling.

In the Middle East there's bags of filthy women,
In the crack or up the back all for a shilling.
Frenchmen pay five francs Doughboys pay a dollar,
You can shoot your cream in the old harem all for a shilling.

Out in India there are no filthy memsahibs,
So what do the pukkah wallahs get for their shilling,
Knotholes in the floor or the hole in the elephant's bottom,
But in Calcutta you can grind in the gutter all for a shilling.

On the ocean waves there are no filthy wrens sir,
So what does poor Jack Tar get for a shilling.
Admirals keep a goat, Captains have a parrot,
But the matelot true has a grand blow through all for a shilling.

THE DUCHESS OF LEE

I had tea with the Duchess of Lee,
She said, 'Do you fart when you pee?'
I replied with great wit that I belch when I shit,
I thought that was one up to me.

I dined with the Duchess of Lee,
She said, 'Will you fuck once with me?'
I replied with great tact, 'As a matter of fact,
I have brought my French letter with me,'

I DON'T WANT TO JOIN THE ARMY

I don't want to join the Army, I don't want to go to war
I'd rather hang around Piccadilly Underground,
Living on the earnings of a high born lady.
I don't want a bullet up my arsehole
I don't want my bollocks shot away
For I'd rather live in England, in Merrie Merrie England
And fritter all my fucking life away — Gawd Blimey!

On Monday I touched her on the ankle
Tuesday I touched her on the knee.
On Wednesday, success, I lifted up her dress,
On Thursday she took me home to tea — Gawd Blimey!
On Friday I put my hand upon it.
On Saturday she gave my balls a tweak
And on Sunday after supper, I stuffed the whole thing up her
And now I'm paying ten and six a week — Gawd Blimey!

Call up the Army and the Navy. Call up the rank and file.
Call up the gallant Territorials, they'll face danger with a smile.
Call up the Boys of the Old Brigade to keep Olde England free.
You can call up my mother, my sister or my brother
But for Christ's sake don't call me.

CONTENTS

CONTENTS

CONTENTS

GENERAL ODES AND DITTIES

CONTENTS

NAVAL ODES AND DITTIES

ADDENDA